FreshStart:
21 Days to Stop Smoking

Dr. Dee Burton has worked in smoking-control programs since 1972. Her special area of expertise is the difficult quitting process. She has designed stop-smoking programs for the American Cancer Society and other major national health organizations.

FRESHSTART: 21 DAYS TO STOP SMOKING is the American Cancer Society's unique, *day-by-day* program—proven effective, specially designed techniques to take you successfully through the crucial first three weeks. The information needs and concerns of someone who has not had a cigarette in seventy-two hours are different from those of the same person a week later. Here, the three hooks of smoking—physical addiction, habit and psychosocial dependence—are addressed as they occur in the quitting process. The innovative *FreshStart* program gives you *only* the information and strategies you need *for each day*. Every chapter contains specific actions and behavior techniques to help you succeed at each stage of quitting and, eventually, to kick cigarettes for good.

You'll achieve all the enormous benefits of freedom from smoking, enjoy the bonus of a lifelong plan to manage future stress, and sustain your mastery over addiction—forever.

THE AMERICAN CANCER SOCIETY'S "FRESHSTART:" 21 DAYS TO STOP SMOKING

DEE BURTON, Ph.D.

Former Consultant on Smoking to the American Cancer Society

POCKET BOOKS

New York   London   Toronto   Sydney   Tokyo   Singapore

An *Original* Publication of POCKET BOOKS

POCKET BOOKS, a division of Simon & Schuster
1230 Avenue of the Americas, New York, NY 10020

ISBN: 0-671-62086-X

First Pocket Books Printing February 1986

18   17   16   15   14   13   12   11   10   9

POCKET and colophon are registered trademarks of
Simon & Schuster.

Printed in the U.S.A.

Acknowledgments

I thank Stephen Gilford, who wrote the script for the video version of *FreshStart,* for his thoughtful contributions to this project.

I thank Jeffrey Nemerovski, who brought us all together.

And I thank the following individuals who have assisted me in a variety of significant ways: Michael Carlisle, Ron Dubren, Edith Grace Hodge, Bobbie Jacobson, Elaine Pfefferblit and Irving Rimer.

Contents

CONTENTS

THE AMERICAN CANCER SOCIETY'S "FRESHSTART:" 21 DAYS TO STOP SMOKING

INTRODUCTION

Getting Ready to Quit

Cigarette smoking is an addiction, a habit and a psychosocial dependency, but it is, in all cases, conquerable. Tobacco smoking is the leading cause of emphysema, lung cancer and heart disease, but stopping smoking reduces one's risk for these, as well as other, chronic diseases. Regardless of whether you've tried ten times before to quit or this is your very first effort, you can stop smoking *now*, for good, and be smoke-free forever.

Consider the facts. Right now, today, there are over 35 million ex-smokers in the United States alone, and 95 percent of these men and women succeeded in kicking tobacco with no professional or outside assistance. We want to make clear from the start that there is no such thing as a person who will never be able to quit smoking. Not only is this statement true, but quite a few ex-smokers even found it easy to stop.

When you ask men and women how they quit smoking, the response you get more than any other is: "I just made up my mind to stop and threw my cigarettes away" or "I went cold turkey, and that was that."

Still, it isn't easy for everybody, and for a lot of smokers, stopping is an extremely difficult process. This *FreshStart* program is intended to enable you, step by step, to make *your* stopping as comfortable a process as possible: a process that will lead to freedom from tobacco forever.

In some ways, breaking the nicotine addiction can be an easier process than conquering other addictive substances. But in other ways, stopping smoking can be significantly more difficult than dealing with almost any other addiction. The myth that tobacco smoking is merely a habit lingers on, leaving most smokers unprepared for any physiological changes they may undergo as part of the stopping process. The pervasive tobacco advertising in our society promotes the illusion that smoking is a habit one can walk away from with ease.

This doesn't mean that stopping smoking is never easy. Clearly, as we've said, it *can* be, and may be for you. And even if stopping is a tough and uncomfortable ordeal, it is certainly achievable. An important premise of this book is that the more realistic your expectations are, the more information you have about the variety of withdrawal experiences that may accompany your stopping, and the more potential obstacles you plan ahead for, the greater your likelihood of success in conquering tobacco. *Plan for the worst and expect the best* is the motto that applies here.

How to Use This Book

This book has twenty-two chapters: this introductory chapter to help you get ready to quit smoking, and a chapter for each of your first twenty-one days off cigarettes. Each day's chapter gives you information and strategies to help you succeed, with as little discomfort as possible, in conquering the cigarettes that—*through no fault of your own*—you have become hooked on.

Each chapter will give you strategies to deal with the kinds of experiences you may be having on that day *and* will also give you strategies to store away for use in the future.

This book is meant to be read one day at a time. It was also written to be read backwards and forwards! By this we mean that from time to time we refer you back to an earlier chapter, and occasionally we give you a glimpse of what's to come in a later chapter. We encourage you both to read this book one chapter at a time in sequential order, and also to use the book as a reference source for particular issues whenever they may arise. Each chapter concludes with a quick checklist that you can use to trigger your memory of that chapter's content.

We suggest you write in this book. Use all four margins or paragraph indentations—wherever you can find white space, please make notes to yourself.

We also suggest you keep your *FreshStart* book with you as much of the time as possible.

And one more suggestion: you'll need a pen or pencil and a few sheets of blank paper. If you fold some paper and insert it into your book for future use, you'll be all set to embark on your twenty-one day program.

Good luck!

Commitment versus Ambivalence

"If you want to stop, you can." This familiar assertion is just not true. *Wanting* to be free of cigarettes may well be an essential step in the stopping process, but it's only one step. The fact that you're reading this book—which is not a candidate for recommended vacation reading—suggests that you're already beyond the wanting-to-stop stage.

How you think about your own wanting to stop can, however, play a role in determining your success. While you want to stop, you may also want to keep on smoking. There are lots of perfectly valid reasons why you may want to stick with cigarettes: the withdrawal process may constitute an interruption, a temporary interference, in your life; avoiding cigarettes is, for a while, going to require energy and attention that you could otherwise focus elsewhere; the cigarettes you smoke may be taking the place of food, thereby helping you to keep your weight down; your life may be filled with stresses and you may want to avoid adding the stress of breaking a powerful addiction; finally, you may find smoking pleasurable.

Wanting to keep on smoking for any of these reasons in no way diminishes the chances of your stopping. In fact, acknowledging these feelings is part of the stopping process. The desire to keep on smoking does not mean you will continue to smoke any more than *wanting* to quit magically transcends the withdrawal process and transforms you into a successful ex-smoker. The point is just that there are very few 100 percent choices in life. It is relatively rare that one choice has only positive attributes and the other choice is completely without attraction to us. In making a commitment to stop smoking the only relevant question is: which do you want more—to smoke or to stop?

Here, then, is the first of a few brief exercises that appear in this book. All of these exercises are short and aimed at moving you forward in the stopping process. You will find no exercises or information here meant only to amuse you and none designed merely to help you better understand your smoking behavior. Our hunch is that you understand the dynamics of your own smoking pretty well, and that it is, rather, the dynamics of successfully stopping with which you'd like assistance.

From Ambivalence to Commitment

To get beyond ambivalence and strengthen your commitment to dumping cigarettes, make two written lists. List One can be titled "Reasons for Stopping," and List Two, "Reasons for Continuing to Smoke."

Start with List One and then go to List Two. Make each list as long as possible. Most important, be completely honest. Include only your personal reasons for wanting to stop or to continue smoking. Don't worry about whether the reasons for either would make sense to anybody else. Nobody else's opinion matters!

Take your time.

Once you've exhausted the listing process for one sitting, put the lists aside, but in a handy location in your home or workplace. As you go about your day's activities, return now and then to the lists, and see if you recall more items you can add. If you like, you can spend a few days on this process.

Once you feel your lists are complete and represent-ative of your current state of thinking on the topic of (ouch!) abstinence from tobacco, take a few minutes to review each list separately.

On List One, draw circles around your top three reasons for stopping. Do the same for List Two: circle your top three reasons for continuing to smoke.

Next, still considering each list separately, place a check mark next to the strongest reason in each.

And finally, compare the two lists. Consider the number of items in each list, but pay more attention to the quality of the reasons in the two lists. Determine which you want more: to stop or to continue smoking.

A decision to stop can be based on a clear-cut distinction—90 percent versus 10 percent. Or it can be a very close call—51 percent versus 49 percent, for example. It doesn't matter how far apart the numbers are. Once you actually stop smoking, the reasons in List One will grow and those in List Two will shrink.

Stopping smoking is itself the way to raise your commitment to a 100 percent level. For now, you can commit to stopping on the basis of the strength of the reasons you've just listed. Having fully considered all of your conflicting feelings, you can put them behind you. There is no need to try to negate or counter these desires to smoke: they are real feelings and will disappear on their own once you've successfully acted upon your commitment to stopping.*

The Three Hooks of Smoking

Almost every smoker is hooked to cigarettes in three ways: habit, chemical addiction and psychosocial dependency. An occasional smoker may only experience smoking as a habit or an addiction. But because of the length of time and the frequency with which most smokers use cigarettes, all three hooks generally apply.

If smoking were only a habit, the number of smokers would by now have plummeted. Nine out of ten smokers in the United States say they want to stop smoking. If simply breaking a habit were the only task facing them, most of them would already have achieved their goal. For most smokers, the habit aspect of smoking is the easiest hook to conquer. For some, the habit is automatically broken once they make it through a few days without cigarettes. For others, a fair amount of attention may be required to break the habit. Steps to accomplish this will be spelled out later on, once you've started your twenty-one day program.

---

* But what if List Two won out? If, for now, your personal reasons to smoke seem more important than your reasons for stopping, jump ahead for a preview of Day Fifteen. Imagine that you've already stopped smoking for two whole weeks as your read this chapter. Then leave your sneak preview and come back to this exercise.

While most smokers are addicted to nicotine, not all of them find conquering the chemical addiction difficult. And difficulty in breaking the addiction is not necessarily related to the intensity of the addiction. The withdrawal process is most difficult for men and women who don't expect it, who are taken by surprise by the physical and emotional symptoms of nicotine withdrawal. Early in your twenty-one day program we will describe in complete detail exactly what withdrawal symptoms can be like. None of these withdrawal experiences are unbearable and all of them have been overcome by many, many smokers who have quit successfully, but they can seem overwhelming if unexpected or not understood.

The most complex and, for many smokers, the most difficult hook to conquer is psychosocial dependency. Note that we are not referring here to a personality characteristic. *The most independent of individuals can be psychologically dependent on cigarettes.* The dependency is a function of the smoking, more than of the smoker. This hook does, however, interact even more with the personality and lifestyle of the smoker than do either the habit or chemical addiction properties of smoking.

Planning ahead, with strategies for each potential obstacle, is the key to success, even *with* the psychosocial dependency hook of smoking. One by one, in the pages that follow, we'll describe each of the ways in which cigarettes foster dependency. And for each example, we will provide a strategy to erase that dependency quickly, sometimes even painlessly!

Selecting a Quit Day

For today you have one major task ahead of you: *selecting a Quit Day*. There is one important fact about this twenty-one day program that you should know before selecting your Quit Day. Namely, Day One of your twenty-one day program *is* your Quit Day.

This *FreshStart* program does not take you day by day through the process of *getting ready* to quit. Rather, the step-by-step process starts with the day you begin your life as an ex-smoker. One step at a time, this program will help you through the mixed trials and joys of your first twenty-one days off cigarettes. During these twenty-one days you will be reading about future strategies to make sure you are prepared to stay free of tobacco forever. Three-fourths of all recidivism—that is, returning to smoking—takes place within the first three weeks after quitting. So, when you complete your twenty-one days of not smoking, you will be in a position of real strength for dealing with the occasional obstacle that may appear in the following months.

Schedule your Quit Day soon. Aim for a day that you expect to be relatively low in stress—and low in opportunities for distraction from your goal. But don't belabor this point: a day of total tranquility is an unrealistic expectation for many busy people. And in the long haul, you will have to deal with stress, temptation and distraction as an ex-smoker, too, though probably more successfully than as a smoker!

Once you've settled on a date, you need to decide

whether to go public with your Quit Day. Here are facts that may be helpful in deciding.

For most smokers, announcing their Quit Day is a positive step, one that strengthens their commitment to stop smoking and encourages their friends to support them when the day arrives. In fact, for some smokers, *not* announcing their intended Quit Day is a step toward self-defeat. A secret Quit Day leaves more room for waffling and reneging.

There is another side to this issue, however. Some men and women work best with private goals: they don't like to discuss their progress and their struggles along the way. If you prefer to work alone toward this goal, that's fine. Keep an open mind, though. Stopping smoking is a uniquely complex experience, and once you're in the throes of it, you may decide that the support of certain friends could be helpful and make a real difference.

Approaches to Quitting

Once you have your Quit Day firmly in mind, you can choose how best to prepare for it. You can opt to go cold turkey, or to prepare gradually.

First, a definition. "Cold turkey" means abruptly stopping. Thus, if you regularly smoke two packs a day, going cold turkey would mean continuing to smoke the two packs or so a day right up until the day before you stop. Then, of course, on your Quit Day, you would smoke zero cigarettes.

The great majority of successful ex-smokers have

quit cold turkey. Partly this fact reflects a difference in degree of confidence between smokers opting to stop abruptly and those preferring to put off stopping for as long as possible! A smoker who chooses a gradual approach may be saying, "I'm not really ready to stop." And even if he or she doesn't start out with this passive attitude, it may evolve as the days roll by. If one has already spent twenty days cutting back on smoking before Quit Day, it becomes easier to add one more day of preparation. And one more day. The significance of Quit Day may diminish as time goes by.

There are even more dangers in a gradual approach to cessation. Once you cut back your nicotine intake to a certain level, you begin to experience withdrawal. And if you continue to smoke at all—even two cigarettes daily—you maintain the withdrawal state. Thus, it is always counterproductive to spend a long time cutting back on your cigarettes in preparation for stopping. If you prefer a gradual approach, two weeks should be your maximum period of getting ready for Quit Day.

Having extolled the virtues of going cold turkey, let's also acknowledge the positive side of the other choice: gradually preparing. If you have never gone a whole day without smoking—cannot even imagine, perhaps, what it could possibly be like—a gradual approach to Quit Day may help build your confidence.

If you generally do your best work by taking small, incremental steps toward a goal, you may want to do the same with the goal of becoming a non-smoker. (In all ways possible, apply success skills you already possess to this objective. And the process of becoming a non-smoker will itself doubtless yield new success skills.)

If you have already tried on many occasions to stop cold turkey and have failed, you may benefit from a gradual approach this time. Perhaps you approach this goal too impulsively, without giving enough thought to the process or the significance of stopping. While you spend a few days preparing to stop, you can use part of the time to reflect on the meaning of stopping—on the seriousness of this goal for you. It isn't only living longer: it's being free from chronic disease; it's the quality of your life that's at stake.

Meanwhile, if you want to go cold turkey, the choice, as we've said, of most successful ex-smokers, you need do nothing to change your smoking pattern. Just keep your Quit Day in mind. Circle the date (no longer than two weeks away) on every calendar you own. Better yet, invest in some new calendars. Mark your Quit Day *everywhere*.

If you want to prepare gradually, here are two approaches that have been successful for some smokers.

Postponing is a method that does not require you to count your cigarettes or remember when you've had your last one. Here's how postponing works.

First, count how many days until your Quit Day. If you have approximately one week, you can postpone cigarettes for two hours daily. If your Quit Day is two weeks away, you can postpone by one hour each day.

Here is how a one-week postponement schedule works. On the first day of your schedule, wait two hours after getting up before smoking *any* cigarettes.

Once you start smoking, however, you can smoke as much as you like the rest of the day—you don't even need to think about keeping track of the number of cigarettes you smoke. On the second day of your postponement week, wait *four* hours after awakening before starting to smoke. Once more, you can indulge as much as you like after the four hours is up. On the third day, wait six hours, and so on, each day waiting two additional hours before smoking. As you can see, by the time you get to the end of your postponement week—to your Quit Day—you will already be going most of the day without any cigarettes.

An alternative gradual approach to Quit Day is the familiar version of *tapering*. You can taper by decreasing the number of cigarettes you smoke each day by a fixed amount for a few days before your Quit Day. If you usually smoke two packs, or forty cigarettes, a day, you could, for instance, decide to cut back by five cigarettes a day for one week before you quit altogether. On the first day, then, you would smoke a maximum of thirty-five cigarettes. You could smoke these any time you like, but not any more than a total of thirty-five that day. The second day of this preparation week you would smoke thirty cigarettes; the next day, twenty-five cigarettes; and so on. On the day before Quit Day, you would be smoking only five cigarettes during the entire day.

As you can see, there are no absolute rules and no magic in either postponing or tapering. The idea is merely to provide you with a structure for cutting back in preparation for Quit Day. If you decide to use a gradual approach to Quit Day, you can taper, postpone or use any method of your own to cut back on smoking. A structure is important, but the particular structure is up to you.

Note that a gradual approach versus cold turkey will make virtually no difference in what the physical aspects of your stopping experience will be like. That is, you can't avoid withdrawal symptoms by using a gradual approach. The most important contribution you can make to the success of your Quit Day—and every day thereafter—is to spend some time reflecting on the result you're after: picture yourself as a successful non-smoker; make that image as real as possible, and enjoy it to the hilt.

Your Personal Statement of Commitment

Whether your Quit Day is tomorrow or two weeks from now, there's an important step remaining in your preparation for it. Obvious though it is, try not to take this step lightly. Many longtime ex-smokers have found it to be the key to their success. We'll be referring back to this step from time to time in this *FreshStart* program.

Think of a sentence—just one sentence—that states as strongly and personally as possible what stopping smoking means to you: what makes you feel good about putting cigarettes behind you. This is meant to be a private statement between you and yourself, only.

You may find that this statement reflects one of the items from the list you made earlier of reasons to stop smoking. On the other hand, this single statement may not have appeared at all on that list. Your statement can express either a reason or a strong feeling. Imagine a statement that two years from now will still ring true for you. Examples of statements are: "I want to see my grandson graduate from college," or "I feel prouder of this than of anything I've ever done," or "I'm not going to die young of a heart attack," or "They said I couldn't do it!"

Write the sentence in your own words on a small card and put it in your wallet *now*.

We'll be talking to you again about your personal statement of commitment as part of your twenty-one day program. For now, we'll leave you to prepare for Day One: your Quit Day. Review the checklist below: it contains all the steps you need to take between now and Quit Day. Think of your personal statement, sit down, relax, and get ready.

GET READY CHECKLIST

1. Acknowledge your commitment to stopping smoking.
2. Pick a Quit Day.
3. Choose to go cold turkey, or to postpone or taper.
4. Write your personal statement; put it in your wallet.

DAY ONE

Quit Day

Congratulations!

The decision to stop smoking is one of the most important decisions of your life. Tobacco smoking is the number one cause of death and disability in the United States. Smoking is the leading cause of lung cancer, emphysema and heart disease. Stopping smoking, *no matter how long you've smoked*, reduces your risk for every one of these and other chronic diseases.

Today may be cold turkey day for you, or it may be the end of several days of gradually cutting down on your intake. All that matters is that today is Day One: Quit Day.

Your day may stretch out before you exactly as you had planned it. Or there may be unexpected twists or turns: maybe you had planned to take the day off, but now you have to go to work after all. Perhaps your child has a cold and must stay home from school. Your car may have broken down; your plumbing may need repair. Maybe you feel under the weather, as if you're finally catching the flu that's been going around.

None of these unwelcome surprises alters the fact that today is your Quit Day. Imagine that today, your personal Quit Day, is a holiday, like New Year's or even Halloween. Think back to all the Halloweens you can recall. There may have been good Halloweens, bad ones, ordinary ones and perhaps an extraordinary Halloween or two. No matter what was going on in your life, though, October 31 was always Halloween. If you woke up on October 31 and found you were fresh out of pumpkins, you couldn't put off Halloween until the next day. You had to go through with it *that day*, with or without the pumpkins.

Consider your Quit Day in the same vein. You can easily come up with a reason—maybe a whole set of reasons—why it's better to wait until another day to stop smoking. Please don't do that. You may not feel prepared to stop today, and that's fine: very few men and women feel perfectly prepared at the start of their Quit Day. The purpose of this program is to help you feel more and more prepared, a little bit at a time, as you gain experience mastering each small or large obstacle that confronts you. *Keep always in mind the fact that this struggle is time-bound.* Stopping smoking may be extremely easy for you or very, very hard—there's no surefire way to predict the degree of difficulty you'll experience. It is absolutely *guaranteed*, however, that the difficulty will end, and end soon. Conquering the hooks of addiction, habit and psychosocial dependency may feel like an interminable process, but it absolutely is not. In fact, for the great majority of smokers the hard part is over within a couple of weeks after they stop smoking. If you are someone who has had a negative experience in the past with stopping—where the struggle lasted longer than a few weeks—we'll be preparing you in this *FreshStart* program to make sure that experience does not happen again.

For now, it's time to work through your first day off cigarettes.

Congratulations for sticking with your Quit Day!

Four Crucial Behaviors

There are several important activities for you to carry out today. If you have a busy day already, take a few minutes right now, read quickly through this chapter and then determine how to restructure your day to fit in all the new non-smoking activities that we'll be telling you about, including reading this chapter again more slowly.

If you have a slow day in front of you, that's even better: this is one day when boredom is not likely to engulf you. You can expand your Quit Day activities into a full day of acquiring new skills—skills to help you stop smoking—and gaining confidence in staying off cigarettes. In your case, too, it might help to read quickly through the chapter—even though you're not in any hurry. Then you can come back and spend as much time with each section as you like.

Do you have your red felt pen handy? Or yellow magic marker or whatever you like to underscore and circle with? Feel free to mark up this book. Draw stars, asterisks, check marks and exclamation points.

Number the paragraphs to fit your interests. Write notes to yourself in the margins. If you have never before decorated a book, here's your chance to let loose.

WATER

It is crucial that you fill up on water today and for the next two or three days *at least*. Fill up in this case means: drink water all day long. Most of the behaviors that make a difference in success in stopping smoking sound either so easy or so obvious that they can be taken for granted. Keeping filled up on water falls in this category. In fact, though, water can do a lot to ease any discomfort on your Quit Day. Here's how:

First and most important, drinking enough water creates a temporary bloated sensation that helps to counter the physical cravings for tobacco you will probably be experiencing for a while. One of the reasons some people overeat when they first stop smoking is to attain that full or bloated feeling that diminishes the craving for cigarettes. Water is more effective than food or other liquids in creating that sense of fullness. And not only does water not result in weight gain, but, by acting as a diuretic, it actually helps in weight control or weight loss—a fringe benefit! If you are someone who ordinarily is not a big water drinker, you may find this is a new behavior you'll want to maintain, even when cigarettes have become no more to you than a distant memory.

Second, drinking water all day keeps your mouth busy: an important point for some new ex-smokers who find they miss the constant activity of puffing on a cigarette.

Third, keeping filled on water keeps you busy in numerous other ways as well, and for many persons in the throes of stopping, keeping busy is essential to their success. Whether you are making quick trips to the water cooler or to the refrigerator or to the faucet, or uncapping multiple bottles or jugs of spring water, these activities (plus stopping off at the bathroom) will give you at least a small sense of purpose during a period when your tendency may be to feel somewhat directionless or unconnected. This unconnected or distracted feeling is a part of nicotine withdrawal for some men and women. We'll talk more about withdrawal later, but for now keep in mind that these feelings will disappear within a few days, as long as: *one*, you ignore them and, *two*, you stay off cigarettes.

Water also helps to speed the nicotine out of your system. *However, all the nicotine will be gone within two days from Quit Day, regardless of what you do* (except use tobacco), whether you drink water or not! The primary significance of drinking water is that it helps to diminish the nicotine cravings that accompany stopping smoking for a majority of men and women.

Sean is a stand-up comic and a successful ex-smoker from New Jersey; he recalls how water helped him during his first few days off cigarettes as follows:

"Perrier was becoming popular in the States right around when I was quitting smoking. I'd heard that drinking lots of water was the way to get off cigarettes, so I started drinking this new, fancy, bottled water all day—I really stocked up on it. My friends all saw me digging it and I started serving it to them, too. Next thing I knew it seemed like Perrier was everywhere: restaurants, bars, supermarkets, even greasy spoons, for crying out loud. To this day, I'm convinced I'm the guy who started the Perrier craze!"

STICK CINNAMON

Stick cinnamon may not ever become one of the grand pleasures of your life, but you'll have to admit it beats snapping yourself with a rubber band (a behavioral gimmick that some smokers use effectively to remind them not to smoke!).

Many of the activities helpful to people who've just thrown their cigarettes away are pleasurable or, at the very least, neutral behaviors. Drinking lots of water and sucking stick cinnamon are not likely *today* to come even close to completely fulfilling your desire for a cigarette, but they do feel *good*.

Are you familiar with stick cinnamon? You may have used it in cooking or have enjoyed it in tea or holiday drinks. For now, we're just suggesting you buy a box or two and try sucking a stick of cinnamon.

Stick cinnamon can be found on the spice racks of your grocery store or supermarket. *A box of stick cinnamon costs less than a pack of cigarettes and it lasts a lot longer.* Here is how stick cinnamon can help you in your first week or two off cigarettes.

There will be no need for a "substitute" of any kind, once you have been off cigarettes for a while. But in your earliest hours and days of abstinence, a temporary oral substitute may make things easier. Stick cinnamon has been found by many ex-smokers to have been the most practical aid in this regard. Here's why.

One, stick cinnamon is extremely convenient, as any aid to conquering an addiction must be. The box it comes in is even smaller than a cigarette box or package. The cinnamon stays fresh for a long time, so one or two boxes will last you through your entire period of breaking the three hooks of smoking.

Two, a stick of cinnamon resembles a cigarette enough in shape and size to be comforting in your first days of non-smoking. But stick cinnamon is so different from cigarettes in other sensations that it will not reinforce any dependency on smoking.

Third, the taste of cinnamon is a fairly uncommon one: a flavor that is unlikely to be associated in your mind with smoking—whereas almost all flavors you regularly enjoy do have this unfortunate link to cigarettes (and we'll be talking more about these kinds of links to smoking in the days to come). So, because the taste of cinnamon is not associated with your smoking, it will not trigger a desire to smoke.

Evelyn from North Carolina told us of her experiences with stick cinnamon:

"Not realizing how long a single stick could last, I went out and bought several boxes before my Quit Day. Stick cinnamon was really helpful to me in my first few days. I guess I must have sucked on cinnamon for almost a month, and then I just forgot all about it until almost a year later—it was my birthday—and my neighbor Gladys gave me a "Cinnamon Cook Book" for my birthday. I must have looked kind of weird—I mean, it was a peculiar present—but then she grinned and said, "I know it's your favorite spice;

you're the only person I've ever met who keeps a cupboard full of cinnamon!"

You may not be certain that you will need a temporary oral substitute to help you through the days that follow. We suggest you buy the stick cinnamon today, as early as possible, and find out *by trying it* how much it helps. Each of the steps to non-smoking suggested in this *FreshStart* program is pretty easy. If you follow up on *all* of them, your odds of being free of cigarettes forever are tremendously enhanced.

PHYSICAL EXERCISE

No, this isn't one of those quit-smoking programs which insists that while you stop smoking, you might as well start an intensive exercise program, go on a diet, get a better job and improve your social skills at the same time (though all of these can be natural accompaniments of your becoming healthier!).

Physical exercise can, however, be a strong factor in helping you to maintain your new non-smoking status with ease and comfort.

Increasing overall exercise in frequency and intensity is an excellent method of combating symptoms of stress. Many smokers use their cigarettes to comfort them and thereby reduce stress symptoms. Smoking is a self-destructive approach to stress management. However, the new ex-smoker who previously has used cigarettes in this regard (knowingly or unknowingly) may initially feel an increase in tension or the experiencing of other stress symptoms. In addition, withdrawal from tobacco can itself be stressful, raising the individual's stress level even higher in the first few days of abstinence.

You can generally reduce your experienced stress level by adding more physical activity to each day. Moreover, you can also combat particular periods of tension or specific stressful incidents by immediately engaging in a period of moderately intense exercise of any kind.

Here is a little more information about the benefits of increasing your physical activity. Over the coming weeks you will find that you are increasingly able to take pleasure in exercise, regardless of whether it's taking long walks, working in your yard or playing tennis.

The known benefits of physical activity for improving your physical health are many. One established benefit is that exercise improves circulation and is therefore recommended as part of treatment for men and women with circulatory disorders. Your circulation will improve automatically when you stop smoking, and so exercising even a little bit more will maximize this improved circulation. For diabetics, both exercise and avoiding smoking are essential. Exercise also plays an important part of the treatment regime, under physician supervision, for individuals who have suffered heart attacks.

And the *number one factor* that can prevent persons who've had a heart attack from having another, possibly fatal one, is stopping smoking. For smokers, conquering their addiction is also by far the most important contribution they can make to *preventing* heart disease. But regular exercise is, to a lesser degree, helpful here, too. Men and women who exercise on a regular basis for an extended period of time are likely to have the HDL (high density lipoprotein) fraction of their cholesterol raised. The HDL is the "good" part of the cholesterol, because it is associated with reduced risk of heart disease.

There also are many known advantages of physical activity that are specific to improving one's mental health. The benefit with the most widespread applicability is that exercise, as we've said, brings relief from the symptoms of psychosocial stress. Exercise is also important in the treatment of depression. It is well known that depressed people tend to become very inactive, and extremely depressed people can become immobilized. But it also works the other way around: physical inactivity can result in depression! Keep this in mind. If you find yourself feeling somewhat down, and your attempts to get in touch with that feeling provide you with no insight as to why you feel that way, consider whether you've been getting sufficient physical exercise.

Physical activity gives you more energy. Think of the people you know who exercise on a regular basis, and then think of those who don't exercise at all. Which group has more energy? The increased energy results partly because your body is working better. When you stop smoking, your heart and lungs become more efficient in their functioning. Similarly, regular exercise makes these organs work better.

You don't need to exercise in order to quit smoking. And in terms of priorities, stopping smoking is by far the most significant thing you can do to improve your health and reduce your risk of every one of the diseases that are the leading causes of death. But as we've said, a little extra exercise may do a lot to help you manage stress in the next couple of weeks. And if there are fringe benefits of that exercise, so much the better.

Here is one specific way in which physical exercise of a particular kind will help you today and tomorrow and maybe the next day.

If you have intense, acute cravings for nicotine (and not everybody does), try this: when you experience the craving, immediately touch your toes ten times or jog in place while you count to thirty.

That's all. The craving will be gone, *and* you'll feel relaxed. (We'll be giving you more information about cravings on Day Two of your *FreshStart* program.)

DEEP BREATHING

As an easy method of countering cravings and of relaxing, deep breathing is tops. But deep breathing can help you even more if you begin now to practice it routinely throughout your day.

First, check to see that you naturally breathe in the healthiest, most efficient manner. *Inhale*. When you inhale, your abdomen should expand. Then, as you exhale it will gradually relax. Is this the way *you* breathe? Some people have developed a habit of breathing in the opposite manner—sucking in their abdomen when they inhale. If you do this, then you'll have the extra reward in practicing deep breathing of learning how to breathe properly. Correct inhalation and exhalation quickly becomes a habit, as it is consistent with your body's natural tendencies.

Here's how to practice deep breathing as a technique to relax.

Inhale strongly, being sure that your abdomen expands to its fullest extent. Then, very, very slowly, exhale. Take at least twice as long exhaling as you did inhaling. You'll feel a natural need to inhale again once you've spent enough time exhaling, but never rush the exhalation.

If you find yourself feeling slightly nervous, fearful perhaps that you won't make it successfully through your Quit Day without a cigarette, sit down for two or three minutes and do nothing but practice deep breathing. Think of nothing else but your body while you inhale strongly, and exhale very, very slowly.

If you have a strong desire for a cigarette that seems as though it will not go away, sit down and practice deep breathing. Watch your abdomen expand and then relax. *Relax*.

Part of the comfort or satisfying sensation that accompanies smoking is the experience of puffing: inhaling and exhaling in a practiced manner. For some people, stopping smoking leaves a void in this regard. A few ex-smokers even find their breathing does not feel right when they first stop smoking. This problem will correct itself in a short period of time. Practicing deep breathing, in the way we've described, however, will solve the problem immediately.

Ritualizing Your Personal Statement

Remember your card with the single sentence stating your strongest sense of what stopping smoking means to you? Go to your wallet and get the card out now.

Part of the power of a cigarette is that it constitutes an *automatic* response. By virtue both of the addictive and habituating nature of smoking, you can be drawn to cigarettes unconsciously. A cigarette can as unexpectedly pop into your hand as it does into your mind. It is therefore extremely important to have another *automatic* response available: one that halts the automatic tendency to smoke.

The four activities we've just discussed can serve this purpose. Keeping filled up on water, sucking stick cinnamon, touching your toes ten times at the first inkling of a craving and practicing deep breathing: all of these will become automatic behaviors that counter any still-present tendency to want to smoke.

The most important automatic response you can create for yourself, however, is through *ritualizing your personal statement*. What does this mean?

To ritualize your statement you can, beginning right this minute, repeat it over and over to yourself. The statement already represents your strongest desire for being free of cigarettes, and it is written on the card before you in your own words.

As you repeat your personal statement, be sure to use the same words each time. As you initially repeat the statement, look at the card and read the sentence. This will help you to ritualize the sentence visually as well as verbally. After you've repeated the statement clearly and slowly, looking at your card, at least a dozen times, repeat the sentence without looking at the card, at least a dozen more times.

By ritualizing your personal statement of commitment in this manner you create a *meaningful but automatic response* that can come to your rescue in moments when you can't quickly enough summon up a conscious roadblock to a compulsion to smoke.

In sum, this easy ritualization process is a way of creating an automatic behavior. Just as the thought of a cigarette can pop into your head without your consciously summoning it, so this personal statement can automatically come to you and overrule the wish to smoke.

This may all sound a little abstract now, but please give it a try. Repeat your personal statement over and over. Then put your card back into your wallet.

Making This Time Unique

If you are like most successful ex-smokers, you've tried to quit more than once in the past, and haven't made it last. You may not have made it through a single day or, worse, you may have made it through a matter of weeks or even months, and then succumbed to cigarettes.

Keep in mind we said most *successful* ex-smokers. Trying to stop smoking and not completely doing so is not a mark of failure, unless you yourself make it so. A few false starts can correctly be considered as practice: practice for the real thing, the main event. Practice implies learning, and it implies improving over time. Therefore, to make maximum use of your previous efforts, take a few minutes now and think about them. What did you learn from those attempts?

Grab a pen or pencil now and make some notes for

yourself on paper, or, preferably, in the margins of this book. What have you learned from your earlier attempts to dump tobacco?

If you're drawing a blank, try the following questions as prompters. Jot down your brief answers: they may seem more insightful on another day than today. What was the longest you ever went without cigarettes? What did the absence of cigarettes *feel* like? Are many of the persons you spend time with smokers? Do the people you live with smoke? Does your lover smoke? Is smoking freely permitted where you work?

What seemed the most difficult aspect of trying not to smoke? If you've tried more than once to quit, how did the various attempts compare with each other? How many times have you *seriously* tried to quit? When was the last time?

Do you drink alcohol on a daily basis? How did that interact with your tobacco quitting? Do you smoke marijuana? On your most recent attempt to stop smoking, where were you when you had that first post-stopping cigarette? Were you alone or with someone else? Who? Do you remember what you were thinking when you took that cigarette?

In thinking about your previous experiences in stopping, you don't need to come up with success stories, strengths or techniques that worked for you. If you do remember successful approaches, great! Jot them down now so that you can use them again if needed.

But jot down also details of hard times: times you felt you needed a technique or aid and didn't have an appropriate one. Note the biggest obstacles to your successful cessation: these are what the *FreshStart* program is designed to help you with.

Here are some of the obstacles that other new ex-smokers recalled when they looked back on their previous attempts to get rid of cigarettes.

Art, a mechanical engineer, remembers: "I'd been off over two weeks and then, by chance, I had lunch with an old girlfriend who was in town. I took her to this really chic restaurant. It was all pretty romantic. She was still smoking, *our* brand, and this terrific wave of nostalgia came over me. To tell you the truth, I don't know if it was for her or for the cigarettes; all I know is I started smoking with her."

Sally, a secretary, recalls: "I was doing fine; I hadn't even gained any weight. It had been over a month. Then this notice came in the interoffice mail announcing that this other woman was the new office manager—the job *I'd* been waiting on pins and needles to hear about. Nobody had even bothered to tell me I wasn't getting it. I just walked into the lunchroom and asked the first person I saw for a cigarette."

Roberta, a salesperson, remembers: "I always did okay at work and when I was out of the house. But I could never make it past a few days at home. My husband smokes, and my cousin who lives with us smokes, and it's just too much to deal with."

The big question now is: how can you make this time *unique*? How will your current effort be different from your previous attempts to stop? You may have some answers to this question based on your thinking about your previous attempts. We'll be offering you a lot of strategies for situations like the ones described above, but as a start we suggest you consider the following:

> *This time will be unique in that*
> *this time you're going to do it.*

This time will be unique in that this time you'll know that a year from now, you'll barely remember the urgency of your current desire to smoke tobacco. Part of attaining success in stopping smoking, as in many of life's challenges, it just to let go of the possibility of failure.

> *This time is unique in that*
> *this time you're doing it.*

This doesn't mean that there will be no slips nor that you will never again puff on a cigarette. You will make this process tremendously easier on yourself if you *don't* ever again take a puff and if you work to avoid slips. But for some successful ex-smokers, slips and slides have been part of the stopping process.

Again, if you've tried before and haven't made it, you're in good company. If, on the other hand, this is your first serious attempt to quit, you have the opportunity for an exhilarating experience: to be home free on your first try. Either way, keep in mind that:

> *This time is unique.*

For now, check the easy steps below and be sure to pursue them all day long today and for the rest of the next week or two.

QUIT DAY CHECKLIST

1. Keep filled up on water.
2. Keep a box of stick cinnamon with you at all times.
3. Touch your toes ten times when the urge to smoke hits you.
4. Practice deep breathing (inhale—abdomen out; exhale—relax abdomen) throughout the day.
5. Repeat your personal statement over and over.
6. Put in the front of your mind: *This time is unique.*

DAY TWO

Withdrawal Symptoms

Breaking the Addiction: What It Feels Like

Congratulations on your successful completion of Quit Day. *Congratulations on being a non-smoker.*

Today we're going to spend a lot of time talking about withdrawal symptoms: because if you have them at all, today and the next couple of days may be when most of these symptoms hit the hardest.

Maybe you haven't experienced anything resembling a symptom of withdrawal and never will: this is entirely possible, even if you've been a heavy smoker. If so, count your blessings and continue to practice the crucial behaviors from your Quit Day checklist.

Nicotine is a powerfully addictive drug. In fact, it has even been reported that when you measure the percentage of users who lose control of their substance intake, nicotine is six to eight times *more* addictive than alcohol!

It is nonetheless true that you *can* stay off cigarettes and that there are ways both to minimize your discomfort in doing so and to make the difficult period relatively *brief*.

Being prepared ahead of time is a key factor in your success in conquering an addiction to nicotine.

Being prepared means, first, knowing that the addiction is a property of the cigarettes—of the nicotine—and not a characteristic of your personality. Being addicted to cigarettes does not in any way, shape or form mean that you have an addictive personality.

Next, being prepared means understanding that stopping smoking may *feel* a little different (or a lot different!) from going on a diet or avoiding a food you've developed an allergy to or, on the other hand, trying to break a habit.

If you're someone who's already conquered another addiction, you know what we're talking about, and you can use the skills you've acquired in your previous experiences to quickly end this addiction to cigarettes.

If, on the other hand, you have not experienced other addictions and are perhaps even surprised to learn that nicotine is a *potent addictive drug* in every sense of each of those three words, then we'd like to take away the mystery for you. Specifically, we're going to describe for you, one by one, each of the symptoms associated with withdrawal from tobacco. Feeling dizzy or light-headed on and off for a few days is nothing terrible—unless you don't expect or understand the sensation. Tingling sensations in your arms and legs are, at worst, the equivalent of being tickled.

But if you think these sensations might last forever, or if you imagine they are symptoms of a major breakdown of your body, they can be terrifying.

You may already have experienced some of these symptoms yesterday or today. On the other hand, the soaring level of your adrenaline as you struggled to resist all temptations of your Quit Day may have sufficed to keep you from experiencing any symptoms! You may have felt nothing but elation so far. That, too, was part of the reason for the "four crucial behaviors" (exercise, water, stick cinnamon, deep breathing): keeping busy can help keep your mind off withdrawal experiences. If that's the case, great! But as your adrenaline dips closer to normal day-to-day functioning, you may begin to notice some unusual feelings, of the kind we'll be describing. *The later you experience withdrawal after stopping, the weaker the symptoms will be.* It is *never* the case that you will successfully make it through an entire month and then be hit unawares by an intense withdrawal period.

Most of your withdrawal period will be behind you ten days or so from today. *All* of your withdrawal symptoms will be completely behind you within a few weeks, regardless of whether or not you've suffered in the process!

Our opinion is that, all other things being equal, given a choice of pain or no pain en route to being free of tobacco, it's best to opt for no pain! Nevertheless, because we think that understanding the worst that can happen to you in the way of withdrawal is a way of eliminating unnecessary discomfort, here is what you *might* experience.

LIGHT-HEADEDNESS

Light-headedness, a slight dizziness or faintness, is a common symptom of withdrawal from nicotine. While you were smoking regularly, the carbon monoxide from your cigarette smoke prevented a healthy supply of oxygen from getting to your brain. Without this carbon monoxide, your brain is now receiving its normal supply of oxygen. Since you're not used to this normal amount, at first you may feel light-headed or dizzy as a result of it: the same feeling people usually get when they are suddenly deprived of oxygen.

This withdrawal symptom won't last long—usually from a couple of days to no more than ten or twelve. Try to experience it in a positive way. Instead of considering the light-headedness as an irritation or distraction, think of it instead as a pleasant high. Imagine your brain cells being clearer, not polluted, with this high as the happy result. This sensation will disappear on its own soon enough, but meanwhile why not enjoy it!

TINGLING

The tingling sensations in your arms and legs are also signs that your body is getting used to functioning in a healthier way than it was when you were a smoker. When you were smoking, the nicotine constricted your blood vessels on a chronic basis so that your circulation was impaired. Now that you've quit smoking, your blood is circulating in a normal, healthy fashion. At first, you won't be used to such glorious normalcy, and so you'll notice the tingling sensations—which are actually signs of improved circulation. This withdrawal symptom usually lasts about two weeks.

INCREASED COUGH

Many men and women cough more when they first stop smoking cigarettes. This also is a sign that your body is repairing some of the damage caused by smoking.

The tiny hair-like structures that line the inside of your lungs are called cilia. They act like a vacuum cleaner to clean out your lungs. Tobacco smoke paralyzes these cilia. As a result of this paralysis, debris accumulates in the lungs. "Smoker's cough" occurs because in the periods (for example, during sleep) when the cilia are working more efficiently, they have to make up for lost time, and this extra effort causes coughing.

Now that you've completely stopped smoking, your cilia are at last working full-time again, and they may have a big job ahead of them. Your extra coughing now means that the cilia are working overtime to sweep away the grime and gook, and clean your lungs up once and for all! The increased cough may last as long as a few weeks, definitely no longer than that.

DRY MOUTH/TIGHT THROAT

Some people who've recently gotten rid of cigarettes find that their mouth feels dry; a smaller number of new ex-smokers find that they're salivating more. These sensations are compensations for the constant inhaling and exhaling of cigarette smoke: you were used to artificially "controlling" the saliva you created through this sucking-in and blowing-out ritual. When you stop smoking, you may initially tend to salivate either a little more or a little less until your mouth once more gets used to being the smoke-free environment it was meant to be.

You may also, as a new ex-smoker, be acutely conscious that "something seems to be missing." Increased attention to the mouth and throat areas, coupled with the general tension that accompanies breaking an addiction, may heighten your experience of changes in saliva secretion. This self-consciousness may also result in a feeling of tightness in the throat. Just ignore these sensations; they will last only a few days.

HEADACHES

Headaches are not uncommon among men and women in the throes of breaking an addiction to nicotine. The nicotine is a stimulant—a very destructive stimulant—and its removal, once it has created a dependency, may temporarily jar the system. Again, the stress of battling an addiction may also exacerbate the headache. Treat this headache as you would any other one: sit or lie down for a few minutes with your eyes closed; practice the deep breathing as we described it; apply a warm washcloth to your brow and eyes for a few minutes. Do whatever you would ordinarily do to help a headache go away (but don't smoke!). However you do or don't treat these withdrawal headaches, they should occur only on the first three or four days.

NERVOUSNESS

Are you nervous? What light-headed, limb-tingling, coughing person with a headache wouldn't be?

Nervousness is fairly common among people who've just tossed their cigarettes away. The physiological aspects of nicotine withdrawal account for part of the nervousness. Anxiety about what these next few days will be like—and whether you'll *succeed* at getting unhooked from tobacco—accounts for another part of the nervousness. Figuring out what to do with those suddenly empty hands gives some new ex-smokers the jitters. And finally, that sudden stab in the stomach that comes with cravings for nicotine *scares* some men and women into a nervous state.

There are two approaches to dealing with these jitters. The first approach is to keep physically busy. Go for long brisk walks. Take large strides, allow your arms to swing freely at your sides, and look straight ahead as you walk. The second approach is to sit still and consciously help yourself to relax. Seat yourself comfortably in a chair and spend a few minutes focusing on the deep breathing we talked about on your Quit Day. This constitutes a relaxation exercise. (Tomorrow we'll teach you a more elaborate exercise.)

Two more considerations about nervousness. The first concerns our earlier advice to you to keep busy. Keeping busy is, indeed, a big aid to the stopping process. Once in a blue moon, however, someone overdoes it. If you find that your constant activity, zipping from here to there and jumping from one event to another, is leaving you frenzied, give it a rest. For some individuals, placing as few demands on themselves as possible is the key to successful cessation of smoking.

Finally, the last point we'd like for you to keep in mind, especially if your nerves are on the ragged edge today, is that people become *calmer* once they stop smoking. It's only a matter of time, but you will surely be a more relaxed person once you're completely free from this nerve-racking drug.

CRAVINGS

CRAVINGS! Of course we've saved this big withdrawal symptom for last. We've mentioned cravings before, and we'll be talking about them again in the coming days. A craving—and not everyone will experience this symptom—is an intense recurring hunger, in this case for nicotine. The craving is sometimes accompanied by stomach pains.

The two most important facts for you to know about cravings are: one, each craving lasts no more than twenty seconds, and two, the craving will go away on its own (always!) no matter what you do.

At their worst, cravings may, in your first few days off cigarettes, recur so frequently that they seem to constitute one big, constant craving. Remember that this one big craving actually consists of several smaller ones: pay attention to where one craving ends and another begins. Once you do this you'll see that you have at least a few peaceful minutes between cravings. Again, you need do nothing to make the cravings go away—in all cases, they will disappear by themselves. And the converse is true, too: there is nothing you can do *wrong* that will make the individual cravings last longer or extend the duration of this withdrawal period, except, of course, one thing— smoke a cigarette.

Remember how we cautioned you in our introduction against spending more than two weeks or so to prepare for stopping by decreasing your cigarette intake? We explained that once you get down to a certain number of cigarettes, to an amount that does not satisfy your addiction, you are maintaining yourself in a constant state of withdrawal. This is exactly what would happen now if you smoked a cigarette to satisfy a craving; you would, indeed, satisfy that one particular craving, but you would increase the likelihood of additional cravings because you would be rekindling your addiction.

One note of reassurance here: even if you do take a cigarette today, it certainly doesn't follow that you're back to ground zero—one cigarette doesn't necessarily erase thirty-six hours of successful abstinence. So, if you have slipped, don't throw in the towel! Just remember that avoiding these puffs here and there will help you to get this whole ordeal over with a lot quicker.

Meanwhile, although you need do nothing about cravings other than resist any temptation to smoke, you can diminish their intensity by keeping filled up on water; and you can relax and take your mind off the cravings by either touching your toes ten times or practicing deep breathing. These easy but crucial behaviors are meant to ease your discomfort and speed you through the withdrawal period.

The cravings are, for everybody, worst in the first week off cigarettes. After two or three weeks, most new ex-smokers feel almost no cravings. An occasional isolated craving may hit you every few days when you've been off cigarettes more than a couple of weeks. The double-barreled danger here is that these late cravings may surprise you when your guard is down, and they may scare you into thinking that you'll always want to smoke. *You will not always want to smoke*. Know that now. We'll be reminding you in the coming days to be on guard for the occasional surprise craving that may arrive late. We'll also be discussing some other withdrawal symptoms that may last a little longer than those discussed in today's chapter.

For today, keep the pointers on the next page in mind. We'll be back with you tomorrow.

DAY TWO CHECKLIST

Keep in the front of your mind:

1. All withdrawal symptoms disappear on their own.
2. The later you experience withdrawal after stopping, the weaker the symptoms will be.
3. Most withdrawal symptoms will be gone within ten days.
4. All withdrawal symptoms will be gone within a few weeks.
5. The withdrawal symptoms are signs that your body is returning to a healthy, normal state.
6. Each craving lasts no more than twenty seconds.
7. Keep filled up on water; touch your toes ten times; practice deep breathing; repeat your personal statement of commitment.

DAY THREE

Relaxing

"Quick—relax!"
"Hurry up—get calm!"

What Is a Relaxation Exercise?

A relaxation exercise is just that: a procedure to help you calm down, maybe even *get mellow*. There are a variety of ways to achieve this purpose. A classic exercise is the progressive muscle relaxation exercise. Throughout this procedure you tense and then relax different parts of your body, thereby coming to precisely appreciate the distinction between tension and relaxation, and learning how to cultivate the latter. Other relaxation exercises involve visual and auditory imagination; in these procedures you shut your eyes and imagine something soothing, such as lying on a golden beach and listening to the waves of the ocean gently lap against the sand. Still other relaxation exercises, like the one we'll be teaching you, involve kinesthetic imaging; in this kind of approach, a sense of movement is the key experience. Some relaxation exercises are based on chanting, and others involve repeating aloud a statement, such as "I am calm."

If you've never done a relaxation exercise, you're in for a pleasant experience when you learn the one in this book. If you're accustomed to doing relaxation exercises of one sort or another, now is the time to do them even more often.

The main purpose of a relaxation exercise is to help you relax your body at will. The exercises can be done with the assistance of another person who leads you through the procedure, or you can listen to a recording of the exercise. In the long run it will be helpful for you to learn or memorize the procedure so that you can recite the steps to yourself and do the exercise whenever and wherever you like.

The eventual goal of a relaxation exercise is to get to the point where you don't need to do one! The idea isn't that you'll become tension-free (an impossibility—you'll have to settle for smoke-free!), but that you'll become able to relax at will, just by saying "relax" or giving yourself some other cue.

Relaxation exercises vary in length, but when you initially start using one it's a good idea to spend about fifteen minutes each time you do it. And it's important, while you're in the learning stage, to practice the exercise at least twice a day.

You might enjoy trying out a variety of these procedures and then deciding which one works best for you. Some people can relax with any exercise, while others have to have one with visual images and still others can only calm down by chanting. The idea, though, is to find one relaxation exercise that you enjoy and to practice that one exercise during the learning stage in exactly the same way each time you do it. After you get it down pat, you can let your mind take you where it will each time you do the exercise, as long as you don't leave the relaxed state.

There is more information about relaxation exercises we want to give you, especially about how they can help you to stay smoke-free. But first, we want to give you a relaxation exercise to learn. Here, then, is the Floating Exercise.

The Floating Exercise

Here's a good way to learn this exercise, which will probably be new to you. First, read through the exercise once to get a sense of what it's all about. Then, go through the exercise step by step, trying out each segment (for example, rolling up your eyeballs, slumping your shoulders, etc.). Read through the exercise two or three more times to memorize it. Don't worry about getting the words exactly right; just memorize the *sequence of events*, and enjoy the experience. Using a tape recorder or having a friend read the exercise to you are also effective ways of becoming familiar with the procedure.

Most relaxation exercises are meant to be done in a seated position, and that's the case with the Floating Exercise.

Ready?

Begin by getting seated in as comfortable a position as possible. Just relax and get comfortable in the chair in whatever position is best for you.

One: Look up toward your eyebrows. Straight up. Now, look even higher toward the top of your head.

Two: While you're looking straight up like this, slowly close your eyelids. Close your eyes all the way. Take a deep breath and hold your breath a second.

Three: Slowly exhale. Just exhale all over until your body feels very limp and relaxed, like a marionette puppet gently collapsing on a stage.

Keep your eyes shut but let your eyeballs relax in whatever position is comfortable for them.

The first thing to do in helping yourself enter into a deep state of relaxation is to close out all of the sounds of the world around you.

Next, get rid of any thoughts you have about anything other than what's happening right then and there, and in particular, what you're experiencing in your body.

Most important, put aside all considerations of time. Imagine instead that you have an infinite amount of time available to you and that the only thing you have to do with all of this time is to concentrate on getting your body more and more comfortable and more and more relaxed. Take your time and relax your body all the way from the top of your head to the tips of your toes.

Begin with your head and let your entire head relax. Notice a pleasant, light tingling sensation in your scalp. This light, tingly feeling is the sensation of tension disappearing from your head.

Let your face relax and feel light. Notice how the lines in your face slowly seem to erase themselves, so that your entire face is now light and tension-free.

Let the pleasant feeling of relaxation spread throughout your head and into your neck. Let the muscles in the back of your neck loosen up gradually, so that your neck feels light and loose and wobbly.

Let your shoulders slump, so that your arms can relax all the way down from your shoulders . . . through your elbows . . . your forearms. Let your wrists feel loose and easy. Let your hands relax, so that your fingers are so light and tingly now that they seem to want to move. There's a feeling of lightness and movement in your hands.

Let your legs relax in the same way all the way down from your hips . . . your thighs. Let your knees relax . . . your calves. Allow your ankles to feel light and loose and wobbly just as your wrists did.

Let your feet feel comfortable and relaxed, so that you become aware of each individual toe feeling lighter than it did a moment ago.

Notice how, as you continue to relax, your breathing becomes easier and easier, deeper and deeper, and requires less and less effort on your part.

First you relax and then you feel light. And you'll know when you're entering into a state of very deep relaxation because the feeling of lightness will spread throughout your entire body.

And finally, you feel so light that you become

aware of what seem to be floating sensations in your body: this is the experience you ultimately want.

You may want to see yourself floating, or you may want to see a light, buoyant balloon floating. But most of all you should get in touch with the *feeling* of floating. It is the feeling of constantly increasing lightness and buoyancy. It's the feeling of lightly and happily floating through space, feeling very light and very easy and very peaceful and very secure.

First you relax; then you feel light; then you float.

When you were very young, when you were just about two or three years old, you couldn't always distinguish between reality and fantasy or between what was true and what was a fairy tale.

Try to recapture this same vivid childhood imagination and use it now to a fuller extent than you have perhaps used it in many years; use it to actively assist yourself in becoming more and more involved in the fantasy of floating, in the feeling of constantly increasing lightness and buoyancy and floating . . . just slowly floating through space, being totally surrounded by space, and completely supported by that space . . . the feeling of lightness and buoyancy and floating, just floating, slowly floating farther and farther away from the rest of the world—lightly and happily floating, just floating.

Three: With your eyes still closed, roll your eyeballs up toward the top of your head.

Two: Slowly begin to open your eyelids, so that your eyes are open all the way.

One: You should feel completely relaxed and alert.

Its Uses for Stopping Smoking

A formal relaxation exercise, such as the Floating Exercise, can extend the kind of experience you get by practicing deep breathing. During your withdrawal from nicotine, each time you sit down and do an extended relaxation exercise, you eliminate a whole series of potential cravings. Practicing relaxation will help to get rid of the nervousness that some new ex-smokers experience in the first couple of weeks off tobacco. Doing this exercise will also take the edge off any anxiety or fearfulness you may be experiencing.

If this is your first exposure to a relaxation exercise, you may be surprised to learn that leading yourself into a state of deep relaxation is a very pleasurable experience—one you may want to pursue even when you're not feeling at all tense or nervous. Since it is so pleasurable, it's perfectly fine to do a relaxation exercise as often as you like, for the rest of your life. Keep in mind, however, that as an aid to managing the symptoms of stress, a relaxation exercise is meant to be a learning tool. Here's how the exercise works in this regard.

First, memorize and spend a few days getting used to practicing the procedure in the manner we've described: at least two fifteen-minute sessions per day. Continue to spend as much time with the exercise as necessary at each sitting in order to enter the state of very deep relaxation you'll quickly come to identify. Once you get used to leading yourself into this deeply relaxed state, you'll find it takes less time to get there on each occasion.

Don't rush it, but once you feel totally at ease in relaxing yourself, try gradually to shorten the exercise. The idea, as we mentioned at the start of this chapter, is that, gradually, the amount of time required for you to relax at will should become less and less. The eventual objective is to get to where you can give yourself a cue (like saying to yourself "relax") and *immediately* experience that state of total, deep relaxation. Once you achieve this goal, you will really reap the full benefits of having practiced relaxation. Anywhere, any time, you will be able to say to yourself "relax" and instantly bring under control symptoms of excess stress.

A few more words about relaxation exercises as aids to stress management. *A relaxation exercise only treats the symptoms of stress,* not the stress itself. The Floating Exercise or any other relaxation exercise helps you feel relaxed in the same way that a Valium or vodka might help you feel relaxed. But a relaxation exercise gives you a drug-free, healthy approach to symptom treatment, one that doesn't have any destructive aftereffects.

When you effectively treat or reduce the symptoms of stress, you are more capable of dealing with the actual sources of stress; this is what total stress management is all about. In the coming days, we'll be giving you strategies to manage a variety of life stresses. These strategies will not be for your use only now; rather, they will be lifelong tools that will help you feel better and be more effective in managing the events of your life.

Meanwhile, practicing the Floating Exercise or any relaxation exercise of your choosing is a grand way to reinforce your emerging identity as a calm individual, free from tobacco. On this, your third day as a non-smoker, you may not yet *feel* this identification with relaxation and freedom. You may very well instead feel overwhelmed. All the more reason to practice relaxation: the Floating Exercise provides a positive step toward letting go of some of the many restraints cigarettes have placed upon your life.

Try it.

DAY THREE CHECKLIST

1. Today, learn the Floating Exercise or any other relaxation exercise you feel comfortable with.
2. Practice the relaxation exercise *at least* twice a day, for fifteen minutes each time.
3. Keep in mind your identity as a calm individual, free from tobacco.
4. Practice daily the "four crucial behaviors" (see your Quit Day Checklist, page 44).

DAY FOUR

Quick Rewards

One of the many special aspects of the feat you're achieving right now is that your rewards from what you're doing today will continue to grow over time. We'll be telling you a lot about these rewards, including the tremendous benefits in terms of huge reductions in your risk for every major chronic disease. But for today we'd like to stick closer to the task at hand: at this instant, you may still be struggling intensely, and any long-term benefit of quitting, however important, may seem a distant and trivial carrot to hold out for.

Here, instead, are some quick rewards—some benefits you've *already* obtained from stopping smoking, and others which you can make happen in a flash. Turn your mind away from the struggle for a moment and focus on the good news. And, if you're *not* struggling, if you've found that dumping tobacco is a lot easier than you'd imagined, so much the better. Lean back, imagine the rewards you've already given yourself, and relish each one.

The first reward: it's gone. If you haven't smoked for the last three days, all the nicotine is now out of your system. And not only nicotine, but the carbon monoxide, too, is long gone. You got rid of all the carbon monoxide shortly after your last drag on a cigarette. As a result, your risk of a heart attack is already reduced; in particular, your risk of sudden death from a heart attack is dramatically decreased because you've quit inhaling large doses of carbon monoxide.

You've begun to help your friends' health already, too. The "sidestream smoke" (smoke coming from a lit cigarette) with its poisonous constituents, including carbon monoxide, is no longer jeopardizing the lives of people you care about. And the smoke from *your* cigarettes is no longer a factor in the itchy, watering eyes, runny noses and scratchy throats a lot of people get when they're around smoking.

By the way, here's a detail you should know: some people, once they quit smoking, begin—perhaps for the first time in their lives—to be irritated by other people's smoking (and we don't mean just psychologically!). It may be that your own smoking provided you with a smoke screen or immunization to the allergic symptoms described above (and we're referring here *only* to allergic symptoms). Now that you've removed your own toxic shield, your healthier body may feel assaulted by the smoke from other people's smoking.

What's the bottom line? It is that this, too, will end. For the most part, these allergic reactions are temporary and, if not temporary, only occasional. Be glad you'll never again be a party to inflicting these irritations onto others. Take note of all the recent policies protecting the rights of non-smokers to breathe clean air; these policies are for you, too. Start checking out places to go that don't allow smoking; ask for a table in a non-smoking area of your favorite restaurant. Find out exactly what the laws and policies governing smoking in public places are in your community. As of this very moment, you can fully enjoy your own right to clean air.

More rewards. Not all smokers experience easier breathing when they quit smoking, but a lot certainly do. Some men and women never realized they had smoking-related breathing difficulties until after they kicked tobacco and felt the difference!

Improved senses of smell and taste are legendary among new ex-smokers. Have you given yourself a chance yet to experience the difference? Try a dish you've previously considered bland; does it taste a little more flavorful today? Try putting less salt on your food; doesn't the food taste better now? You might even want to indulge in a new cologne—or your first cologne, if you don't ordinarily wear any. You can buy it with the money you've saved from your four days of non-smoking!

More energy? Well, yes, of course. Over time your energy supply will, indeed, expand; all you'll have to do is allow yourself to experience it. You may already be starting to feel more energetic, though not neces-sarily. The withdrawal period may still be in your way (don't worry, it won't be cramping your style much longer). Now is a good time to start testing your energy. Start a brisk walking program. Or play your favorite sport a little more often, and a little longer each time. Choose one of those dreary household chores you've been putting off and give it your best shot; maybe you'll get it done this time. If you do find you have more energy today, that's terrific—but, be assured, this time next week, you'll have even *more* energy.

What we're saying in this chapter is that some rewards of stopping smoking (like living longer and living healthier) come to you automatically, no matter what. Other rewards need to be helped along a little. You won't notice your improved sense of taste if you keep dumping salt on your meals; you won't know how much more energy you have till you stand up, reach out, and try to use some of it. Being free of cigarettes *is* its own reward, but you can still create some extra rewards. Why not go for the gold ring?

DAY FOUR CHECKLIST

1. Focus, today, on all the rewards you've *already* reaped as a result of stopping smoking—nicotine gone, carbon monoxide gone, risk of heart disease reduced, irritation of sidestream smoke to family and friends gone. *Add your own rewards.*
2. Help along some rewards—flex your muscles to test your energy, try new foods to enjoy your keener sense of taste, buy your favorite person a new cologne with the money you're saving.

DAY FIVE

Triggers

So far we've talked mainly about the chemical addiction hook of cigarettes. Physical symptoms of withdrawal do not affect all new ex-smokers, but their impact is immediate for those men and women who are affected. Withdrawal may hit hard or not at all, but if it does strike, it's in the first few days without cigarettes. Of course, you know this already, either from having read the earlier chapters of this book or—alas!—from personal experience. The good news is that, either way, if you've made it to Day Five, the worst physical symptoms of withdrawal are behind you. Today, we're going to talk about cigarettes' second hook: *habit*.

Smoking is a habit. Brushing your teeth, crossing your legs after sitting down, straightening your glasses, putting cream in your coffee, stopping your car for a red light, saying "hello" when you pick up the telephone, eating popcorn in a movie, saying "excuse me" when you step on someone's foot, and smiling when you see a person you recognize—these are also habits. As you think about these examples, you can see that some of these behaviors are highly desirable, others are neutral, and some may be bad habits.

A habit is a behavior that, through repetition, has become automatic. Breaking a habit requires attention in order to avoid the automatic, or habitual, response. For instance, imagine that a one-way, east-bound street in your neighborhood is converted to one-way west-bound. In the past, as you approached this corner (let's call it Ames Avenue), a traffic light, a stop sign or some other landmark may have been a cue to you to get ready to turn right. These visual cues were not experienced on a conscious level; rather, they were signals to your subconscious that triggered a specific behavior, namely turning your steering wheel to the right. You did not make a conscious decision to turn right; you turned right out of *habit*.

Now, though, Ames Avenue goes west instead of east. Your habitual response (turning right) could get you into a lot of trouble. To break this habit, you need to *pay attention*. Hopefully, there will be road signs that help you out by calling the change of direction to your attention.

Here are two essential points about breaking a habit that can be seen in the Ames Avenue example. First, although the results of *not* breaking the habit could be tragic, the process of breaking the habit is, in effect, no big deal. The same is true of your smoking habit.

Second, although you may have been turning right on Ames Avenue twice daily for twenty years, it certainly won't take you another two decades to get used to circling the block and turning west. It will take perhaps a few days of conscious effort (i.e., attention) and then your old right-turn habit will disappear. This, too, is true of your tobacco habit.

Your smoking habit is more complex than your Ames Avenue right-turn habit, but that doesn't necessarily make it more difficult to break. We'll explain why shortly, but first here's a full description of smoking as a habit.

A habit is formed by the repeated association of two events. Thus, the repeated association of Ames Avenue with turning right led to a *habit* of turning right on Ames Avenue. Your cigarette smoking is associated with not just one but many events in your life (as though you didn't know!). Some common links to cigarette smoking are: drinking coffee, drinking alcohol, eating sweets, talking on the telephone, finishing a meal, pausing to relax, experiencing anger, starting your car, ending lovemaking, reading a book, and finishing a chore. Take a minute and think of the events or situations in *your* life that always seem to trigger a desire to smoke. But only take a minute: it may be mildly interesting to consider the dozens or maybe hundreds of links to your smoking, but this information isn't needed in order to break your smoking habit.

Each of these links, then, is itself a habit. Take the first example, drinking coffee: having a cup of coffee triggers a desire for a cigarette. Your smoking, then, is a multi-determined habit; after so many years of smoking, just about everything in your life can be linked to cigarettes, and dozens of events can trigger a wish to smoke! *However*—and here's the important information for you to know about breaking your cigarette habit—you don't need to break all of these links or mini-habits in order to stop smoking. That would truly be a long, roundabout route to cessation. Once you go for a while without cigarettes, all these individual links disappear on their own! *The smoking habit extinguishes itself once you've been off cigarettes for a few days or weeks.* The exact time varies depending on the nature of your habit.

Now that we've made our point so forcefully, we'd like to give you some qualifiers. Of the many links to your smoking, there may be a few that are stronger triggers than others. Today, on your fifth day of non-smoking, you're in a good position to determine what the big links may be for you. That is, after more than four days of abstinence, the cravings (if you've had any) should no longer seem constant, and so you will be better able to single out just what events trigger your desire to smoke. If there are two or three events that prompt more intense desires for smoking than others, you may want to speed your habit-breaking by countering these triggers.

You counter a trigger or link to smoking by changing some part of your habit. If the trigger is coffee, temporarily alter your coffee-drinking habit. If you usually take your coffee light, drink it black for a few days. Or switch to tea this week. Or, if you always drink your coffee from a china cup, switch for a while to a paper cup or plastic mug.

Making changes such as these is effective in two ways. First, when the trigger itself is changed, it has less power because it is less associated with smoking. A china cup of coffee with milk may have been strongly linked to smoking, but a plastic mug of tea with lemon will be only distantly connected.

Second, these changes you make are cues to you, too. For example, the plastic mug of tea with lemon signals you that there's something different going on. The change becomes the road sign telling you: "No right turn on Ames Avenue" (i.e., "No Smoking"). You won't need to read the road sign many times before the message completely sinks in, but in the beginning it's a helpful reminder.

For example, Jesse, an Internal Revenue Service field representative, was surprised to find that talking on the phone was the most potent trigger he encountered. Jesse has a very structured, tightly timed work schedule, which begins first thing in the morning when he sits down at his desk and, within one hour, places between twenty-five and thirty phone calls. He used to chain-smoke throughout this entire hour.

Jesse did two things to counter this trigger. First, he moved his chair to the opposite side of the desk: this was his reminder to himself that things were going to be different from now on. Second, he created a pinboard to log the geographic locations of the contacts he made over the telephone; this new physical activity—searching the board and placing pins—replaced the activity of smoking during his morning hour of phone calls.

Again, however, you don't need to give your attention to countering all of these triggers to smoking. All links will disappear once you've been off cigarettes a little longer. But if there is any link that is giving you a particularly tough time, do use the to-break-a-habit, change-a-habit principle to counter it.

Before we close for the day, we need to mention one link that has a powerful, destructive impact on some smokers, and that's the link between alcohol and smoking. If you drink alcohol, here are some points to keep in mind. First, the alcohol-cigarette link is common and is associated with, among other things, anxiety in social situations. When you're holding a drink *and* a cigarette, you hardly have to worry about what to do with your hands! Second, alcohol is a depressant and nicotine is a stimulant, and the interaction of these two drugs somewhat balances each other experientially and comes to be associated with relaxing. This drink-smoke link thus tends to be a very strong one. Worse, though, the alcohol diminishes your capacity for making sound judgments—in a nutshell, it makes it harder for you to resist the temptation to smoke.

Occasional social drinkers can handle this problem in one of two ways. You can opt to avoid all alcohol in your first few weeks off cigarettes. Or you can counter the triggering impact of alcohol by both watering down and icing up your drinks for this period, and by using the to-break-a-habit, change-a-habit principle.

Heavy drinkers find it extremely difficult to stop smoking. This is especially unfortunate because there is a synergistic interaction between alcohol and tobacco—the damage to health done by alcohol is multiplied many times over by smoking. If you are a frequent heavy drinker, you have a drinking problem and should seek help in dealing with the problem. Don't use your drinking as an excuse to avoid stopping smoking. Dealing with your drinking problem may, however, have to come first. Use this period of time to get rid of substance abuse in your life once and for all.

The link between marijuana use and tobacco use is less common than that between alcohol and tobacco use. However, some smokers do use tobacco cigarettes to try to prolong the high of marijuana or to fill the void between joints. If this is your habit, you have three options. The first and healthiest choice is to dump grass at the same time that you dump weeds. Second, you can choose to just avoid marijuana in these first several weeks off tobacco. And third, you can alter the ritual of smoking marijuana in order to reduce its association to smoking tobacco.

DAY FIVE CHECKLIST

To Break Your Smoking Habit:

1. Just don't smoke! (The habit links will quickly disappear on their own once there's no smoking to reinforce them.)
2. Note any triggers that are particularly bothersome. Counter these triggers with the to-break-a-habit, change-a-habit principle.

DAY SIX

Some Other Withdrawal Experiences

The experiences we'll describe today affect only a minority of men and women who stop smoking. If you have not begun to experience any of these problems, relax; on this, your sixth day of non-smoking, you're unlikely to run into any new withdrawal surprises that will knock you for a loop. Some emotional ups and downs, concentration troubles, sleep disturbances: these constitute the remainder, the last batch, of events arising from withdrawal from tobacco. If you haven't encountered any of these difficulties, please read this chapter anyway, but please do *not* read it with an eye to being on guard. We've asked you and will continue in the next couple of weeks to ask you to plan ahead and be on guard in a number of ways, but not today.

These secondary withdrawal symptoms will not suddenly appear from left field. Instead, if you are not troubled by any of these experiences, read this chapter with an eye to better understanding how tremendously complex and *individualized* stopping smoking is. In the years to come, you will have friends, people you love, maybe even your children, struggle to stop smoking. It will be important to share with them your personal experiences in stopping. But it will be equally important, in helping your friends, for you to communicate that you understand that *their* stopping may be very different from *your* stopping; indeed, theirs may be an even tougher challenge.

If you *have* been troubled with your emotions, sleep or concentration, read on. Although these withdrawal symptoms do not affect the majority of persons, they are far from rare. These problems, when they strike, can be alarming, but rest assured they are ultimately harmless.

Emotional Ups and Downs

GOING HAYWIRE

Has it felt as though your whole emotional makeup has gone haywire in the past few days? Your emotional experiences may encompass more than tension, anxiety and nervousness. Specifically, do you laugh and cry—not just easily, but almost involuntarily? Moreover, do you burst into tears one second and follow it up with a giggle? Maybe it hasn't been all *that* bad for you (it's not for most people), but you do sort of know what we're talking about: you've been feeling oddly on edge, irritable and a tad more *emotional* than your usual self.

What psychologists call "emotional lability" is the problem here. This means that your emotions are easily triggered and can swing from one emotional extreme to the other. Of the various forms that this withdrawal symptom takes, the most common is weepiness. Here is the essential information to enable you to deal with this symptom.

First, emotional lability like all symptoms of withdrawal is temporary and will disappear on its own—you need do nothing to make it go away. You can, however, ease the burden placed on yourself during these two weeks or so of emotional lability by the way in which you relate to the problem.

The best way to handle these "loose emotions" is to indulge them. If you feel like crying, cry. Holding in the tears will only make you tense. Similarly, if you're angry, let out a good yell: express the feeling. There are, of course, some commonsense qualifiers to this principle. If you're an automobile mechanic and you suddenly feel yourself boiling over like the car you're working on, it might be good to put a temporary lid on your anger, rather than blasting the customer sitting in the car. Similarly, if you're an executive in a board meeting and find yourself feeling weepy over ledgers, it might be prudent to stifle your natural inclinations till you get a chance to be alone to weep.

Do, however, allow yourself plenty of time to be as alone as you need to be to cry, scream or growl. The more you release these feelings, the sooner they will be out of your system. Also, as you indulge yourself in, say, "crying over nothing," you will see that there is nothing to be frightened about in these apparently irrational episodes. You will find that the emotional agitation disappears and that you feel calmer once you've expressed the feelings.

The reaction of Sandy, a mother of four from Arkansas, is typical of people who experience this withdrawal symptom. She remembers: "I was scared to death when it first started happening—I'd just start crying. I thought I was going to be a basket case without cigarettes. Then someone told me the same thing had happened to her and it just lasted a few days. I decided to give it to the end of the week. It was like knowing someone else went through the same thing made it okay for me to cry, too, so that's what I did. Then the funny thing was once I had a couple of crying jags, it was all over. I felt great and the whole thing went away."

There is a second point to consider if you've been feeling tearful this week: you may also be missing your cigarettes as though you're mourning them as friends. We'll discuss this in full when we get into psychosocial dependency, nicotine's final hook, later on in your *FreshStart* program. For the next few days, though, just observe yourself in this regard: if you allow yourself to express freely any weepy feelings, they should diminish and maybe even disappear by the end of next week. But if the sadness lingers when the tears are gone, there's more going on with you than physical withdrawal from nicotine. In the chapter for Day Sixteen we tell you how to handle loneliness for cigarettes: if you think this is a major problem for you now, feel free to jump ahead and read Day Sixteen. But please come right back here and join us, as soon as you're done.

A final note on emotional lability: anyone you're

truly close to—your partner, child or best friend—should be advised (warned, perhaps!) of the experiences you're going through. Just tell them straight: "Look, I'm going through withdrawal from tobacco and for a couple of weeks I may be acting screwy. If I yell at you, don't take it personally. If I sob at supper, don't worry about me. I'll be back to normal in no time."

Concentration Troubles

Difficulty concentrating is a fairly common occurrence among men and women who've just stopped smoking. This withdrawal symptom seems to hit hardest the very people who are most dependent upon concentration ability in their work. Individuals who work with constant deadlines, those whose work requires a great deal of organizing, ordering and focusing, and anyone who does either a lot of reading or writing: these are the men and women who are most likely to notice concentration difficulties in the first couple of weeks after they stop smoking.

Difficulty concentrating has its origins in physical withdrawal from tobacco. The experience seems in part to be related, like the symptom of lightheadedness, to the removal of carbon monoxide and the resulting healthier supply of oxygen available to the brain: the brain requires a few days to balance its functioning. In part, the concentration troubles may be due to the removal of the stimulant function of the nicotine. This requires not another stimulant to replace the nicotine but time for the brain to revert to a healthier manner of responding. Finally, to the extent that the new ex-smoker is anxious, the anxiety itself can make it difficult to concentrate.

The antidote for the concentration problem is simple: ignore it. Accept the fact that you're not at your concentrating best today and may not be up to peak mental performance for another ten days. What often happens is that the person finding it hard to focus or concentrate panics, and falls into a state of anxiety—thus becoming truly unable to concentrate! This is analagous to what some professional writers refer to as "writer's block": a writer has a bad day or two, or maybe a bad week or two, in which ideas don't come or words don't flow. This is perfectly normal, but if the writer is terror-stricken by the absence of words, this anxiety state can prolong the void. Hence the feeling of being "blocked."

The panic, then, explains why it's generally the people who most need to be able to concentrate who are hit hardest with concentration difficulties when they stop smoking. It's not really that these men and women are more prone to this withdrawal symptom, but that they are more vulnerable to it and more likely to notice a problem in concentrating and be upset by it.

Again, the key to solving the problem is to ignore it; it will disappear on its own. Meanwhile, for today, here are some tips for helping you to concentrate a little better. *One,* take frequent breaks from your work for brief physical activity. This doesn't have to be strenuous exercise—washing the dishes or walking the dog is fine. *Two,* if you're up against a deadline or if you have a mammoth project to complete, forget the ultimate goal for now. Instead, divide your work into small blocks of time—perhaps one-hour blocks—and then focus only on the one block that you are working on. *Three,* drink skimmed milk for its calming effect as you work. It's much easier to concentrate when you're feeling calm. *Four,* if you ordinarily drink coffee or any beverage with caffeine, that's all right; however, watch your intake to be sure you're not overindulging. Too much caffeine can make you nervous and thus interfere with your concentration.

Sleep Disturbances

Have you found yourself sleeping a couple of extra hours a night? Or, have you been waking up bright and sunny an hour before your alarm is set to go off? Or, maybe you've been waking up at brief intervals *during* the night. On the other hand, perhaps you've suddenly found yourself turning and churning instead of falling asleep at all! Sleep disturbances affect only a minority of ex-smokers but the experiences of those affected cover the gamut of possibilities. Here, again, the most important fact to bear in mind is that this is only a brief, temporary alteration in your sleep pattern. This is a withdrawal experience and will correct itself within two or three weeks. The most helpful guideline in the meantime is to sleep when you feel like sleeping, and if you're not sleepy, get up and do something enjoyable.

Sleep changes, like concentration troubles, can be aggravated by too much attention. For the next week or two, don't count the number of hours of sleep you get. If possible, *don't* set an alarm: sleep till you wake up. If that's not a realistic alternative, and you're feeling very heavy-lidded lately, then go to bed earlier in order to satisfy your need for extra sleep this week.

If your problem is the opposite, and you're waking up before the rest of the world—be happy! You can get a jump on the day and have more time than usual to do the things you enjoy. If you find it hard to fall asleep, you can read a book, watch television and drink skimmed milk. If you feel restless during the night, get up, walk around and involve yourself in a household activity or hobby. Put some photos in an album or arrange your records in alphabetic order. If you cannot sleep *at all,* lie down, shut your eyes and *rest,* without intending to sleep. Lie on your back and stay still; practice deep breathing as you lie there. (Have you been remembering to practice the "four crucial behaviors" for managing withdrawal? Can you name these four behaviors now? If not, turn back to your Quit Day chapter!) Rest will not take the place of sleep on a long-term basis, but it can pinch-hit for a short period. And, as we said, any changes in your sleeping pattern resulting from withdrawal from nicotine will be short-lived.

There is one exception to the statement we just made, but it's a positive exception: quite a few men and women, because they are *healthier* when they dump tobacco, actually come to require less sleep than they previously did! For instance, as your circulation improves with the removal of nicotine from your system, you'll need to sleep less. Similarly, the increased supply of oxygen that comes with the removal of carbon monoxide will help your heart and lungs to be more efficient in their functioning and thus to need less rest at night.

Victor, a New York playwright participating in a quit-smoking group, had successfully quit smoking, made it through withdrawal and was feeling fine— except that he was very worried about his new sleeping habits. He complained that, no matter what he tried, he now woke up at least two hours earlier than he had before he quit smoking. And not only that, but he woke up feeling alert and wide awake as though he'd had a full night's sleep. But when the other group members asked him how much sleep he'd gotten before he quit smoking, Victor replied: "The normal amount, about ten-and-a-half hours."

DAY SIX CHECKLIST

1. The key to handling emotional ups and downs, concentration difficulties and sleep disturbances is: *ignore the problem*. It will correct itself within the next ten days or so.
2. Whenever practical, indulge the feeling: if you feel like crying, cry; if you feel like sleeping, sleep.

DAY SEVEN

One Week Off Cigarettes!

Congratulations! No, the battle isn't over, but being off cigarettes for one week is a major achievement. You're over the worst phase of *physical withdrawal* from tobacco. Any withdrawal symptoms you may have experienced will be less frequent in the week ahead of you. Not only that, but you're also well on your way to having broken the *habit* hook of smoking. If you haven't had a puff in a week, then many of your links to cigarettes have been weakened and are already on their way to self-extinction.

Is this the first time you've gone a whole week without smoking? If so, you really should celebrate; you may not be home free, but you're way beyond first base. On the other hand, are you someone who's made it through a week on more than one occasion, only to succumb to cigarettes at a later date? As we said before, people differ in what part of the stopping process is most difficult for them. We'd like to refer back to Day One—your Quit Day chapter, where we talked about making this time unique.

If you've had previous early successes followed by relapses, please consider these two ways of really making this time unique. One, do allow yourself to feel proud of having been off cigarettes for a week. It doesn't matter that you've done it before—it's still a genuine achievement. Congratulate yourself—you deserve it. Two, focus all your energy on preparing ahead. Do you repeat several times daily your personal statement of commitment to permanent tobacco-free living? You should do so; this is a significant aspect of preparing yourself for unexpected events and feelings. And, prepare yourself for the *expected*, too. Let's face it: if you've stopped and started again more than once, you must have some clues as to what led to your recidivism (returning to smoking). Shut your eyes and think about these earlier experiences; then plan ahead how you will master each of these obstacles should they appear again. A large part of the rest of this *FreshStart* program is devoted to just this aspect of becoming free from tobacco forever, so be assured help is on the way. We'll be suggesting a variety of strategies for planning ahead in the coming chapters.

Now that you've been off cigarettes a week, we'd like to tell you to relax: we'd *like* to, but we can't quite give you a green light on relaxation just yet. Instead, we suggest you relax a *little*, but keep your guard up. What sometimes happens is people are so justifiably thrilled about stopping and so confident that the battle is won that they relax completely, letting their guard down in the process. Now, for many men and women, there's no problem in this—the first few days are the whole deal. Once they make it through a week, it's as though they had never smoked. If this is you—hooray! (But please read the rest of this book so that you can understand that the stopping experiences of your friends and loved ones may be quite unlike yours.) However, other new ex-smokers are knocked for a loop if they let their guard down after a week of success. A stranger at a party may offer you a cigarette and the next thing you know you're smoking it, without ever having made a conscious decision to take the cigarette! Or, you have your first alcoholic drink in a week and a sudden urge to smoke hits you: an urge you're unprepared to conquer because you've let your guard down completely.

John, a filmmaker in San Francisco, had been off cigarettes a week or so and was at a meeting, seated at a round table with a group of colleagues, one or two of whom smoked. He was explaining to his friends in great detail how successful his quit-smoking method had been. As he talked, much to everybody's amazement, he took a cigarette from a pack on the table and lit it. "I don't even think about cigarettes," he continued, completely unaware that he was smoking.

We don't want to alarm you unduly. The automatic smoking responses, if they occur at all, happen only in the first couple of weeks after stopping. (And in John's case, he was less prepared than most individuals to block these impulses consciously, because he had used hypnosis as his method for stopping. Some people do successfully kick cigarettes forever through hypnotherapy; but the method does not emphasize conscious control and planning ahead, which are vital factors in most ex-smokers' successes.) We do, however, want to alert you to the need for vigilance for another week.

An odd thing has happened with some men and women who quit smoking. They quit, for perhaps a week, and felt at ease with their success, but just to make sure they were free from tobacco, they decided to test their success by having a cigarette. In all cases, these were people who had been strongly motivated to stop in order to demonstrate that they were not slaves to cigarettes, that they were *in control*. But somewhere along the way the desire to conquer became more important than the thing being conquered. Like the compulsive womanizer who loses interest once the woman has been won, this person loses interest in staying off cigarettes once the initial victory has been achieved.

If you identify at all with these individuals, if you have any inkling of an intention to test your power over tobacco by lighting up a cigarette, please hear this one message loud and clear: the only way to demonstrate that *you* are in control of cigarettes is to *refuse* to smoke them.

A related but more common occurrence concerns the "occasional cigarette" issue. Some individuals, once they start feeling comfortable without cigarettes, begin to believe that they are immune to smoking's hooks and that they can therefore have an occasional cigarette, perhaps on special occasions. Shirley, the vice president of a Manhattan bank, put it like many other *former* ex-smokers: "I didn't *need* cigarettes anymore, so I assumed I could just have one." Here are the facts on this issue.

It *is* possible for former regular smokers to become

occasional smokers or smokers of two or three cigarettes a day. It's possible in the same way that it's possible to survive a major air disaster, though your odds are better at surviving the plane crash. What happens in 99 percent of the cases in which previously regular smokers have tried to smoke occasional cigarettes is, of course, that they relapse: they very quickly return to their usual number of cigarettes, and then have to put forth the energy *again* to get rid of cigarettes (at least with a hard-learned lesson to benefit them). The special occasions for which they'd been waiting to smoke started occurring with great frequency. Indeed, life became a constant holiday, with special occasions deserving cigarettes all day long.

There's still more to this "occasional cigarette" issue. The rare individual who does manage to pull this off does it only at the expense of expending great energy every single day. The energy that might be put into seeking new challenges, working productively, adding stimulation to a relationship, developing a talent or solving a problem instead goes into keeping one's cigarette intake down.

It may be that you know someone who is only a "social smoker," a man or woman who smokes perhaps only one or two cigarettes every couple of days. If so, think back over the time you've known the person: did they ever smoke more than that? Most likely not. It's the fact that they've never been hooked that permits them to make the choice of being an occasional smoker: a choice that, of course, still lowers their life expectancy, reduces the quality of their life and damages the health of everyone near them.

This, then, is the final point about occasional cigarettes: there is no such thing as safe smoking. One cigarette a day increases your risk of every leading major chronic disease.

Does all of the above mean that if you slip and smoke one cigarette, you're a goner? No, not in any sense of the word. But if you permit yourself to smoke one cigarette "now and then," you're likely to become a goner, because one slip is very different from a cigarette now and then. As we've said earlier, if you have a weak moment and take a drag off a cigarette, don't exacerbate this mistake by belaboring it. There is a helpful maxim for withdrawal from tobacco: *reward successes, ignore slips*. Don't fixate on that one mistake; focus instead on all the puffs you *didn't* take this week. How many cigarettes have you *refused* to smoke in the past week?

Do you have any plans for tonight? We suggest you plan a small celebration: something comfortable, where you can indulge yourself and relax while staying—for just a few more days—on guard against all temptations to smoke.

DAY SEVEN CHECKLIST

1. Reward yourself for being off cigarettes for one full week.
2. Relax a little, but stay on guard for unexpected temptations.
3. Commit to refusing occasional cigarettes or drags.
4. Reward successes; ignore slips.

DAY EIGHT

Rationalizations

There are four stages to stopping smoking: thinking about stopping; making the decision to stop; stopping; and staying stopped. And here's some great news: of these four stages, you've already completed three. You were thinking about stopping before you read this book; you've probably been thinking about it for years. You made the decision to stop, and you followed through on it. Many smokers never get beyond thinking about stopping; they never make the decision. And quite a few other smokers decide to stop but, unfortunately, never make it through the first few days of withdrawal.

The rest of this *FreshStart* program will be dedicated to the fourth and final stage of successfully dumping tobacco: staying off. To help you get off on the right foot in this final turn of the track, we'll begin by talking about rationalizations.

A rationalization is a special form of lie; it's not just an excuse. To rationalize is to give a plausible but untrue motive for one's actions. Some rationalizations for smoking are so familiar that they're clichés. Other rationalizations are quite inventive, reflecting perhaps the desperation of the person to justify smoking a cigarette. What does all this have to do with you?

It's true: you made your decision and did not succumb to rationalizing your way out of stopping smoking. Still, there are two stages where rationalizations tend to spring up and interfere with progress. The first is in making the decision to stop. And the second is in the early part of the fourth stage, the staying-off stage—just where you are now. Why should that be the case?

There are several reasons why a rationalization might seem to come in handy now. First of all, this whole stopping process may be taking considerably longer than you expected it to. The first week may have had an exciting edge to it—doing battle with withdrawal—but the continuing need for vigilance may be becoming a bit tedious. Or you may not be getting the attention you thought you'd get for stopping; compliments may be sadly slow in coming in. Or you may not feel any better. Or you may feel *worse*.

One of several steps in avoiding recidivism, in ensuring that you'll stay off cigarettes forever, is to rid your thinking of rationalizations. This is also an important step in the lifelong process of strengthening character, so you're in for a major fringe benefit by learning to shoot holes in your rationalizations.

Here are several rationalizations. Some of them are bound to sound familiar. Here, too, is an exercise you may enjoy. *Take each rationalization and correct it.*

Restate it, so that you are telling the truth about the topic, instead of rationalizing.

Rationalizations

1. "My mother lived to be ninety-seven and smoked every day of her life, so I don't need to stop smoking."
2. "I'm gaining weight—I told you so!"
3. "I've proven I can do it!"
4. "I've proven I *can't* do it!"
5. "I can't go on like this."
6. "I'm driving my wife/husband/kids/boss/friends/mail carrier crazy."

The above list is derived from the many rationalizations that smokers and new ex-smokers alike have come up with. Can you think of others you've heard? What about your own thinking? Do you have a reason to return to smoking? Chances are extraordinarily high that if you think you have a reason, what you really have is a rationalization.

How did you do in correcting the sample rationalizations?

1. "My mother lived to be ninety-seven and smoked every day of her life." The corrected thought might be, for example, "I can't count on being as lucky as my mother; great genes are rarely enough to compensate for cigarette smoking." Or the corrected thought might be: "There's an exception to every rule. My mother was the exception; I might not be."

2. "I'm gaining weight." Weight gain is a common rationalization for returning to smoking. In fact, there

are men and women who allow themselves to gain considerable weight in order to have a visible, if not valid, reason to indulge in tobacco again. This motive operates at varying degrees of consciousness among different people. Still, even when they truly don't want to, many people *do* gain weight when they stop smoking (your Day Ten chapter coming up soon is devoted entirely to weight management). So if it's a real problem, then what makes this excuse a rationalization instead of a valid reason for smoking? The statement is a rationalization because the weight gain in this case represents a self-fulfilling prophecy. The corrected thought might be something as straightforward as: "I'm gaining weight; I'd better go on a diet."

There are several factors that can lead to weight gain among men and women who've recently stopped smoking. We'll go over each factor in your Day Ten chapter to prepare you to nip these tendencies in the bud.

3. "I've proven I can do it." The person who returns to smoking because she's already proven she can do it is like the person we talked about earlier for whom conquering cigarettes became an abstraction instead of a real goal. The person who uses this rationalization is likely to be someone who is having, in fact, a very difficult time doing it, is missing cigarettes, and wants to assure herself that if she ends up going back to smoking she'll be able to stop again. The corrected thought here might be: "I prove I can do it by staying off."

4. "I've proven I *can't* do it." Some of you may have had an especially tough time last week; you may have had so many slips that you don't really feel you've

succeeded in stopping smoking at all. If so, you may be particularly vulnerable to this rationalization. This one can take many forms—do any of these sound familiar? "I can't quit because I'm an addict" or "I've tried every method there is, and nothing works for me" or "I've had professional assistance and even that didn't make me stop smoking."

The corrected thought for any of these examples could be "I'm having a tough time, but I can do it." If this is your situation, by the way, don't think you have to start again from scratch: that, too, would be a rationalization. Review quickly, in one sitting, the earlier chapters of this book. Focus on the two or three principles that seem most relevant to your own experiences, and then return to this chapter, following through day by day. Today is the eighth day of your quitting experience, regardless of how many slips you've had. Try to have fewer slips today than yesterday, and to have none at all tomorrow. Spend a little time really thinking about why you stopped. Get out your list of reasons for wanting to stop and review them. You've put a lot of energy into the program: stick with it. The tough part will soon be over.

5. "I can't go on like this." An example of a corrected thought here can be, "I *can* go on like this, at least a few more days." And the reassuring news is that you won't have to go on like this much longer. If yours has been an especially uncomfortable withdrawal from cigarettes, remind yourself that the worst is over; in fact, almost all of your withdrawal period is over.

6. "I'm driving everyone crazy." Not only has there never been a single documented case of anyone going

crazy as a result of stopping smoking, but there also is no known case of anyone—mate, friend or mail carrier—being driven crazy by someone else stopping. It's great to be considerate of other people's feelings, and two good ways to be considerate of people who care about you might be, one, to take care of yourself and two, to try to share what you're going through with them. You could, for instance, tell your son or boss, "I'm in the middle of stopping smoking; bear with me—it will get better." And the corrected thought in your own mind for the rationalization "I'm driving my cat/lover/cousin crazy" is: "They understand what I'm going through."

If you're an individual who never permits yourself to rationalize, then you're a very likely candidate for success in becoming free from tobacco forever: by now you may already have attained that freedom. The way in which people think about the process of stopping and staying off is a strong factor in determining their success. It's not that the difficulties of stopping are all in one's mind. On the contrary, there are tangible and potent obstacles to stopping smoking. Not only that, but some men and women have very real life stresses and little support for their stopping efforts. But these obstacles point to the necessity of acquiring a structure and techniques to make stopping smoking easier, such as your "four crucial behaviors," *and* of making your thinking work *for* your success, instead of against it.

If, like many people, you do rely on rationalizations from time to time, try shooting holes in your rationalizations. Each time one occurs to you, correct it in your mind just as you corrected the sample rationalizations in this chapter. Use a complete sentence to correct each rationalization. (There isn't, by the way, a particular type of person who rationalizes. Some people rationalize because they tend to be too easy on themselves. But other people rationalize because, in certain ways, they are too hard on themselves; they don't permit themselves to acknowledge difficulties or to fail.)

In general, getting rid of rationalizing as a way of thinking will benefit you in important ways in addition to helping you to stay off cigarettes. Consider, for instance, that getting rid of rationalizations will encourage you to assert your right to certain pleasures; to enjoy things with no apologies to yourself or to anyone else (i.e., no need for excuses). Second, getting rid of rationalizations will make it necessary for you to confront problems and to make progress in life by changing some of your behaviors. And getting rid of rationalizations will lead you to greater self-acceptance. When you rationalize your behavior, it means you don't accept yourself as you are.

DAY EIGHT CHECKLIST

1. Look for rationalizations in your thoughts about staying off cigarettes.
2. If you discover rationalizations, correct them one at a time.
3. Correct a rationalization by creating a complete sentence that states the truth of the matter, with no excuses.

DAY NINE

Planning Ahead

Planning ahead is the key to staying off cigarettes. Planning ahead may have been helpful in deciding to stop and in stopping, but here in your final stage of successful cessation is where you'll gain most from advance preparation.

The first step in planning ahead is to identify any potential obstacles to staying off cigarettes. Right now, make a list. Take a couple of blank sheets of paper this time, instead of using the margins of this book. Draw a line down the middle of each page. On the left side of your paper, list all the obstacles you can think of— anything at all, big or small—that might thwart your success.

Here are four approaches to help stimulate your thinking and make sure you don't overlook any possible stumbling block. *One*, think of any temptations, frustrations or unexpected occurrences that have presented themselves in these nine days of non-smoking. Include in your list any obstacles you've successfully mastered as well as those you may have fallen prey to. Include, too, obstacles you've never encountered personally but have heard about or imagined. Accordingly, *two*, think back to your previous attempts to stop smoking. Above all else, be sure to list any events that actually led you to return to smoking. *Three*, remember conversations you've had with friends, stories you've heard about what made the going tough for other people. Unless you can say with absolute certainty that these events could never have relevance for you, include them in your list. *Four*, use your imagination. You cannot predict the course of the road that lies ahead, but you can imagine some of its likely contours. How do you expect to be spending your time in the next few months? What could go wrong? How would that relate to your staying off cigarettes?

Make your list of obstacles as long as possible. The more advance preparation you do, the more likely you are to succeed in staying off cigarettes. And the more you plan ahead now, the less you will have to think about in the future. The idea isn't that these are obstacles you will need to keep in the forefront of your mind. On the contrary, once you develop and rehearse a strategy for each potential obstacle, you can put it out of your mind: you've prepared for the situation. Which brings us to the next step—developing a strategy to counter each obstacle.

On the right side of your sheet, jot down a strategy that you are confident will successfully enable you to master each obstacle. You can use a shorthand notation to write the strategy, but be sure that you've given enough time to thinking about it first. Be sure you have some confidence in every strategy you list. Note that there are several possible strategies for handling almost any obstacle, even especially difficult ones. You might, for instance, have entered as a potential obstacle: "My husband returns to smoking." There are a lot of strategies that could help you master this potential obstacle to your staying off cigarettes.

One strategy, for example, would be to focus your energy on supporting your husband in his efforts to quit again. A second strategy, if your husband chooses to continue smoking, is to work out an agreement that one room of the house be designated as a smoking room for his use. A third strategy might be to remind yourself of your own personal success in being free from tobacco and that returning to smoking yourself would mean the loss of a great personal achievement.

As you can see, strategies for mastering obstacles can be actions you take alone, or actions you take with other people or simply a matter of *thinking*. We'd like you to try to think of one or more meaningful strategies for each obstacle on your list. Be as thoughtful as possible in completing this list of strategies, and then hang on to your list! There may be obstacles on your list that you're not sure how to deal with. If so, don't worry; in the chapters to come we'll be giving you a lot of strategies for mastering a variety of obstacles, beginning with strategies for weight management in the next chapter.

Meanwhile, there's a third step to planning ahead that you can complete now for every strategy you've listed, namely: rehearsing the strategies. The idea of a rehearsal is twofold: one, to be sure the strategy is credible, and two, to be sure it's clear in your mind. To rehearse a given strategy, simply close your eyes and imagine yourself in the situation, using the strategy to master the obstacle. Does the strategy seem realistic? Do you understand how to go about doing it? Keep your eyes shut till you feel confident that you can use this strategy to counter the potential obstacle. If you're not convinced it will be effective, put a star next to this item on your list to indicate that it needs more work.

We'll call your attention to your "Planning Ahead" list again. The idea is that as you learn additional strategies in your *FreshStart* program, you can go back and enter them where appropriate in your list.

If you haven't yet completed your list of obstacles and strategies to the best of your ability, please try to do so today.

DAY NINE CHECKLIST

1. List all potential obstacles to staying off cigarettes.
2. List at least one strategy for each obstacle.
3. Rehearse each strategy.

DAY TEN

Weight Management

This is the day quite a few of you have been waiting for—or perhaps you haven't waited, maybe you jumped right here from the Table of Contents! If so, please return to the book's Introduction as soon as you've digested (oops! bad choice of word) this chapter.

First, some information that may surprise you: *most people don't gain weight when they stop smoking.* This is an important fact for you to know. On the other hand, a lot of people do gain weight, and learning that they're in the minority no doubt makes it that much worse for them. In fact, close to 25 percent of smokers gain weight after they stop smoking, and the majority of these gain ten pounds or more. So there is no denying that weight gain is a real threat to many people stopping smoking.

The good news is that weight gain doesn't *automatically* follow giving up cigarettes. And for those who do gain weight, there is nothing mysterious about the reasons why this happens. It isn't a shift in metabolism that accounts for most weight gain, nor is it compulsive overeating. Rather, there are several factors, relating to the process of stopping, which increase one's tendency to put on weight. The key to managing your weight while stopping smoking is to determine which of these factors apply to you.

This is not an exercise to help you understand your eating habits. Rather, the point here is that the different smoking-related factors that can lead to weight gain require different strategies to counter them. As we go over each of these factors, think about these past nine days and note whether you've experienced any of the tendencies described. If you've already gained a pound or two, pay even closer attention.

Food as an "Oral Substitute"

Quite a few people, when they first stop smoking, feel a need to put something in their mouths to replace cigarettes. Note that this is a temporary experience; there is no need for any long-term substitute. But in the first few days off cigarettes, some men and women start grabbing snacks here and there all day long to try to fill this need. This snacking would present no serious problem were it not for the fact that any kind of eating activity can so quickly become a habit. The extra pretzels, buns and bagels that at first were meant only to help one through tobacco withdrawal can become a regular eating pattern.

Think about your feelings and eating activities over the past nine days. If you think you have any tendency to use food as a temporary oral substitute for cigarettes, identify right now a no- or low-calorie substitute for food. Remember the stick cinnamon? If you haven't bought any yet, now's the time.

Food as a Reward

It's terrific to reward yourself for stopping smoking! We hope you'll continue to reward yourself for each milestone you pass (for example, you're now on your way to your second week off cigarettes). However, if you rely on food as your way of rewarding yourself, you could be unnecessarily creating a weight problem. It's not that you have to become an ascetic just because you've stopped smoking. But it doesn't hurt to take a few minutes now and reflect on these past nine days to be sure you're choosing the best kinds of rewards for yourself in the long run.

Some men and women feel a need to compensate for the restrictions they're placing on themselves in resisting smoking by letting go a little more than usual in other ways. This feeling is perfectly valid and could be harmless, as long as overeating doesn't become a pattern. If you think you may be tending to overdo the use of food as a reward for not smoking, take a few minutes now and write down some nonfood rewards. Use the vivid childhood imagination that you use in practicing the Floating Exercise (see Day Three) to help you think of pleasurable rewards. For instance, consider using the money you're saving from not buying cigarettes for something frivolous. Indulge yourself by soaking in a bubble bath for as long as you like. Go see two movies at two different theaters in one day. Sleep late on Saturday. Go dancing and really let go!

Eating to Calm Nerves and Reduce Cravings

You've probably noticed by now that the "four crucial behaviors" play a role in weight management as well as in countering withdrawal symptoms. Another smoking-cessation factor which can lead to weight gain is eating to acquire a full sensation in order to reduce cravings for nicotine and withdrawal jitters. We talked about these feelings in your Day Two chapter and suggested that you keep filled up on water as a way of reducing cravings. By now your cravings should be significantly diminished, if not gone for good. If you find, however, that you still tend to seek food to attain a comforting, full sensation, do two things: one, continue the frequent water drinking even though cravings for nicotine may be gone and two, add large quantities of raw vegetables to your diet. Any and all kinds of raw vegetables—the more variety the better. Don't replace your usual foods with these; rather, use them to supplement your regular (pre-stopping smoking) eating pattern. This roughage will give you the physical comfort you seek during this period. And if these abundant crunchy veggies should become a lifelong habit, so much the better! Eating a variety of fresh vegetables will also help protect you against diverticulosis, heart disease, diabetes and several forms of cancer.

Adding Sweets

Some new ex-smokers report a specific yearning for sweets. Sugar seems to become an irresistible temptation in these early non-smoking days. Aside from strengthening your resistance, you can use several other strategies for countering this tendency toward indulging your sweet tooth. The first is to seek out sour foods when you feel a need for something sweet. It may seem odd, but some people find that a sour taste will satisfy the desire for its opposite. Second, use fresh fruits as your source of sweets as much as possible. Third, if you really want something in the pastry family, opt for a chewy cookie which will take you longer to eat for fewer calories than a big slice of cake or pie will.

Better Sense of Taste

Some new ex-smokers tend to eat more because, without cigarettes, they find they can taste more. It may be that you've always loved rich, spicy foods, but now that your senses of smell and taste are improved, a slice of plain bread really blows you away. If this is the case, the strategy for weight management is simple: eat a little more of these plain foods you can now enjoy and a little less of the richly gravied, sauced and buttered foods you've always liked.

Healthier Appetite

Aside from enjoying the taste of food more, you may tend to eat more because you're really healthier now. Some smokers are frankly malnourished and maintain their weight at the expense of their health. If you're eating a healthy, varied diet now that you're a non-smoker (lots of fresh fruits and vegetables, whole grains and skimmed-milk products, smaller amounts of fats) and you're still gaining weight, physical exercise could be the strategy you need. Increase the frequency and duration of your favorite sport, and gradually increase also the intensity (how fast or hard you play the sport). If you don't have a favorite sport, you can walk away the calories. Consider this: you burn up 100 calories with every twenty minutes of brisk walking. Walking two miles burns up just as many calories as jogging two miles.

Physiological Changes

Finally, of course, there are the physiological changes that take place when you stop smoking. A very small percentage of men and women make absolutely no changes in their eating patterns when they quit smoking but still gain weight. (This has been estimated at five percent of smokers, but the available data on this are not conclusive.) The precise physiological mechanisms accounting for this unexplained weight gain have not yet been determined. What this means, if you are in this very small group of people, is that you will have to exert a little more control to keep your weight where it is. But dieting or drastic changes in your eating habits are not necessary, even in this case. Most people find that adding exercise is the most pleasurable way of managing weight. Consider this: if all other elements in your eating style remain as usual, and you eat just one buttered muffin less each morning and add one half hour of brisk walking daily, you'll have this possible problem well under control.

If you don't seem to be putting on any weight or if you're thin as a rail and would welcome a few more pounds—terrific! Keep an eye on yourself in the next couple of weeks, however; and an eye on the scale wouldn't hurt, either. Remember that most people— about 75 percent—don't gain weight when they stop smoking. For those who do tend to gain, there's a reason behind every tendency. And for every reason, there's a strategy.

DAY TEN CHECKLIST

1. Single out any specific tendencies you may have that lead to weight gain. These include:
   - Food as an oral substitute
   - Food as a reward
   - Food to calm jitters and reduce cravings
   - Yearnings for sweets
   - Improved taste
   - Healthier appetite
   - Physiological changes
2. These different tendencies require different strategies. Use the ones suggested in this chapter or develop your own, but remember: *use the strategy that applies specifically to the tendency.*

DAY ELEVEN

Mastery

Mastery involves having so much skill or knowledge that one is in command of a situation or subject. A desire to be masterful is what motivates some men and women to stop smoking: they want to master conquering the addiction, the habit, the dependency. We'd like you to think about yourself in terms of this issue. Consider how often you feel in control of a situation, not in the sense of dominating other people, but in knowing how to handle the situation and feeling confident you can do what needs to be done. A sense of mastery can relate to stopping smoking in several important ways. Consider which of the following apply to you.

First, mastery you've acquired in earlier experiences can be applied now to the process of becoming free from tobacco forever. Is stopping or staying off cigarettes a tremendous struggle for you? Do you feel you're not in control of the process? If so, think back right now to experiences with which you've been successful. Any kinds of experiences: getting your real estate license, learning to ride a bike, eliminating nail-biting, overcoming stage fright. Think of this successful experience, and allow yourself to dwell for a moment on the feeling of mastering a situation or event. Next, try to remember the events leading up to it. How did you go about it? Did you leap in and deal with the situation all at once? Or did you take small, incremental steps? Were you patient and easy on yourself? Or did you relentlessly push yourself? Whatever process worked for you then can work for you now. Take the mastery you learned from this previous achievement and use it now to help yourself become free from tobacco forever.

There's a second possibility: maybe you cannot recall ever mastering anything. Perhaps you often tend to feel that you are ineffectual, aimless, not in control. If you do feel this way, consider first if you're being fair to yourself. Sometimes people don't just downplay, but actually overlook, their own achievements. They recognize as achievements only events in certain limited categories like careers or sports, for example. If you do feel you've had limited experience in mastering events, then stopping smoking will be a twofold triumph for you. First, you're doing it: mastering conquering cigarette addiction and dependency. If you've made it this far—to your eleventh smoke-free day!—you must be doing not just one, but a lot of things right. The second part of your triumph is that you can take the sense of mastery you've achieved through stopping smoking and apply it to future life experiences.

This mastery, which will continue to pay off for you in many ways, is the third way in which mastery relates to stopping smoking, and it applies to everyone, regardless of how much or how little you've felt in the past that you were on top of situations.

This is a good time to reflect on the elements of the past ten days that have helped you to stop smoking and remain off cigarettes so far. Ask yourself one particular question: "What are the things I did that made a difference?" There is a tremendous range of possible answers. Some of your answers might be old reliable standards like: "I drank water all day," "I did deep breathing," or "I kept remembering my personal statement of commitment." Other answers might be more individualized, such as: "I made a promise to my son," "I did spring cleaning," or "I flew a kite all day the first day."

Think of as many things as you can, and then consider what kinds of actions they were. You can classify the actions any way you like; some classifications might be: seeking support from others, doing something physical, reflecting on the issues involved, making a public commitment, and so forth. All of these represent categories of skills. The idea here is to become aware of the ways in which you're mastering smoking so that you can apply these same skills to future experiences of all kinds.

And congratulations on mastering eleven days off cigarettes. Parties don't always come on weekends, and neither do quit-smoking celebrations. Why wait for two weeks? Why not celebrate eleven days tonight—eleven days of being off cigarettes?

DAY ELEVEN CHECKLIST

1. Apply mastery learned from earlier experiences to stopping smoking.
2. Use stopping smoking, in turn, as a way to acquire new mastery.
3. Apply mastery learned from stopping smoking in other life experiences.

DAY TWELVE

Getting Good Support

The further away from your Quit Day you get, the less relevant the chemical addiction hook of smoking becomes and the more heavily psychosocial factors weigh. In the last chapter we talked about one of several psychological factors involved in stopping smoking and staying off cigarettes, namely the feeling that you are mastering the process. Today, we want to talk about an issue involving your interaction with other people. For many people, the support of others plays a significant role in their staying off cigarettes. But the opposite also occurs: sometimes interaction with other people can lead back to tobacco.

The people you spend time with in this first month or two can make a difference. In some cases, at home and at work for example, your choices may be limited. Here are some guidelines both for those limited-choice situations and for areas of your life where more alternatives are available. First, spend as much time with non-smokers as possible. Has this been your inclination in the past twelve days? If not, consider your motives.

It may be that you've felt so confident about conquering cigarettes that you haven't felt it necessary to avoid smokers. Or it could be that you have deliberately been spending as much time with smokers as possible in order to "inoculate" yourself against the possibility of future temptations. These are constructive choices and, as long as you're staying off cigarettes, it's fine to stick with your original way of doing it. There is another possible motive, though; occasionally someone will seek out the company of smokers because they expect to backslide at some point, and when that happens they want to be in the company of people who are less likely to make them feel guilty. If you think that this might be your motive, resolve to reverse it now before you fall victim to a smoking environment. Use the tips in this chapter to help you make constructive choices in seeking support in staying off cigarettes.

If there are a half dozen people with whom you socialize on a regular basis, and two of them smoke and four don't, schedule a few more dinners or golf games with the non-smokers this month. You can catch up with your other friends next month. The idea is certainly not to exclude or ostracize your smoking friends. However, if the choice is merely one of juggling social dates for a few weeks, why not juggle them in favor of your non-smoking program? Most new non-smokers, like yourself, find it's helpful in the first month or two to spend as much time as possible in a non-smoking atmosphere.

If you live with a smoker, you're in a difficult situation; there's no doubt that this can make your ordeal significantly harder. A caution, however: don't use anyone else's smoking as a destructive issue during this period. Your smoking or not is ultimately a separate issue from anyone else's smoking, no matter what their relationship is to you. Does this sound contradictory? The point is that although a wife or husband who smokes can make your stopping process more difficult, the constructive approach is to deal with the situation as another obstacle and develop strategies for handling it, just as you would with any other stumbling block. Remember that twelve days ago you, too, were a smoker. It probably took you a considerable amount of time to arrive at the point when you actually decided to eliminate smoking from your life. Give the people you care about the right to find their own time and way of stopping. Once you've been off cigarettes a little longer and feel completely comfortable with your own freedom from tobacco, it will be important for you to share your experiences with them, gently encourage them to stop smoking and support them in their efforts. But right now you may not be detached enough from your own efforts to be objective in helping even the person you love most.

Meanwhile, do try to negotiate smoking areas of your home, ideally only one room, so that at least part of your home environment can be smoke-free. After dinner, if a family member lights up a cigarette, don't remain at the table. Take your after-dinner tea or coffee to the living room. Or skip the beverage and take a leisurely after-dinner walk in the neighborhood; this is a wonderful, healthy habit that's good for digestion. Perhaps you can even entice your mate to accompany you for a non-smoking stroll.

At work, don't congregate with the smokers on coffee breaks if there's another alternative. These are not lifelong changes, just temporary ones to ensure your permanent success in non-smoking.

Sticking close to non-smokers is only one helpful tip for this period of time, however. (And as we've said, this tip applies to most new ex-smokers, but not all: do anything you like as long as you're confident you're acting in your own best interests.) Which people to seek support from is another important issue.

If the stopping process continues to be extremely difficult for you, or even if it's generally easy but you're hit every now and then by an almost overwhelming desire to light up, talking to a supportive person can be helpful. In seeking support at this time, be selective in whom you go to. Your best friend or your partner or your mother may be good choices, or they may be the worst possible ones! What is crucial is that the person you seek support from helps you to use your strengths to master any obstacles and resist any temptations to surrender again to cigarettes. At the same time, a supportive person needs to understand that the stopping process is complex and can be difficult. A person whose sole opinion on the subject is that "it's all a matter of willpower—just go ahead and do it!" is not a constructive source of support. Similarly, a person who lacks patience or who berates you if you're slipping and sliding is not someone to share the process with! If they initiate a conversation on the topic, tell them straightforwardly, "I don't want to talk about it now. I'll let you know when I'm ready to discuss it."

How you ask for support can be as important as *whom* you ask for it. If you walk up to a friend and say, "I'm going to die if I don't have a cigarette right this second," you're likely to get an answer like "Go ahead and do it; one cigarette can't kill you." This is not constructive support, but it's the kind of response your statement called forth. Consider instead that you walk up to the same friend and say, "I feel like I'm coming apart, but I don't want to smoke; I need your help." In this case you've asked for support in a way that enables your friend to be more constructive in giving it. There is a key statement that can be helpful in seeking support from others: "I want you to help me stay off cigarettes."

DAY TWELVE CHECKLIST

1. Spend as much time as possible with non-smokers this month.
2. Seek support only from persons you expect to call upon your strengths.
3. Be constructive in how you ask for support.

DAY THIRTEEN

Assertiveness

We said we wouldn't suggest that you try to "make yourself over" just because you're becoming a non-smoker. We meant it. Still, there are benefits to other areas of your life (we've mentioned some, like more stamina, improved senses of smell and taste, a sense of mastery and so forth) that naturally accompany stopping smoking. And there are other important benefits which you can actively pursue with more effectiveness now that you're a non-smoker: some of these also reinforce your success in not smoking. Becoming more assertive is one such change.

The experience of stopping smoking is highly individualized, and this issue may or may not apply to you. Your personal assertiveness may be right on target! Some smokers, however, have difficulty being assertive and use cigarettes to suppress their thoughts and feelings. The business of finding and lighting a cigarette, and then inhaling and exhaling the smoke, distracts them from what they are feeling. When they stop smoking, therefore, they have the choice of either finding another way of suppressing their feelings (an unhealthy choice) or becoming more assertive. From the most positive point of view, then, a fringe benefit of stopping smoking is that it provides an opportunity for greater self-expression. When you get rid of cigarettes, you may at the same time be getting rid of a mask.

First, three definitions. Being *passive* means having difficulty expressing thoughts and/or feelings, and being *assertive* means being able to express thoughts and feelings. The phrase "being able to" is included in this definition for an important reason: one does not have to express one's thoughts and feelings continually on every one of life's incidents in order to be an assertive person. An assertive individual may choose from time to time to leave opinions and attitudes unexpressed. An *aggressive* person, on the other hand, is also able to express thoughts and feelings, but tries in the process to dominate others. A desirable objective for both passive and aggressive individuals, then, would be to become, instead, assertive. Of course, we are not talking here about "personality types," but only about tendencies. People vary in their degree of assertiveness in different situations. Still, we all tend more in one direction than another and most people, on reflection, can identify themselves as being characteristically "passive," "assertive" or "aggressive."

As we said, a lot of smokers have become used to inhaling on cigarettes instead of expressing their thoughts or feelings. Most commonly, cigarettes are used in this way to suppress anger. The result is that the unexpressed anger festers even deeper until the feeling itself may be cut off: an unhealthy habit.

If you find that you continue to experience a great deal of emotion even after three or four weeks, this may be a clue that you have been using cigarettes to suppress feelings. (In the first two or three weeks the heightened emotions could just be withdrawal experiences.)

If you'd like to improve in expressing your feelings more freely, try the following: One, identify one or more people you trust to support you in this endeavor, people with whom you feel free to be vulnerable. Talk to these friends as frequently as possible while you are in this stage of learning to express your true feelings. Begin by describing the most recent emotions you can recall. Don't be surprised if when you first talk about your feelings, you seem unable to experience any at all. This often happens, and is partly the result of the artificiality of the situation and partly because the experience is new to you. Remembering earlier emotional experiences can help you to start feeling as well as talking. You can ask your friends to just listen silently or talk with you about the emotions you're expressing, whichever seems more helpful.

Two, consider adopting a principle of better-late-than-never in communicating an emotional response to someone. People who have trouble expressing their feelings often have a delayed response in experiencing the feelings themselves. Someone may make a remark which doesn't disturb you at the time. But a few hours later you realize suddenly it's made you angry. You may suppress the feeling because now it's too late to express it to the person who provoked it. As a learning process, however, it can be tremendously helpful for you, whenever possible, to seek out the person afterward and communicate the emotion you experienced—for example, "Your remark last Thursday made me angry."

Again, the idea is not that you should make a confrontational issue out of every trivial incident in your life. Rather, this is a way of learning how to become more spontaneous in experiencing and expressing feelings. If you adopt this better-late-than-never principle, what tends to happen is that, over time, any delay between an event and your emotional response to it will become shorter and shorter, until finally you're experiencing your emotions spontaneously.

To become more assertive in expressing your thoughts and feelings, you might want to try some of the guidelines below.

One, try using phrases like "I think," "I believe" and "in my opinion" when talking. This shows that you take responsibility for what you're saying (an assertive position), and that you know the difference between opinion and fact. Consider the following remarks.

Janet to Alan: "Dogs are smarter than cats."

Jim to Ruth: "Space exploration is the frontier of the future."

Both statements have in common that they equate opinion with fact. In presenting an opinion as fact, you seem to be denying the other person the right to express a differing opinion. You run the risk of bringing conversations to a standstill or turning them into nonproductive arguments rather than energetic debates. Without realizing it, you may be cutting off lively discussions and getting less feedback and stimulation from others: you miss out on possible opportunities to learn from the world around you. Think of the difference in tone attained by the modifications in the remarks below.

Janet to Alan: "I've always found dogs to be smarter than cats."

Jim to Ruth: "I believe that space exploration is the frontier of the future."

Two, try to use short, simple sentences. The shorter and simpler, the more likely are your thoughts to be understood by others. And the shorter and simpler, the more likely are your thoughts to be direct and honest: there's less room in a short, simple sentence for evasiveness and hiding.

Three, look the person you are talking to in the eyes: this helps both of you make contact and understand what's being communicated. It's easier to continue being assertive when you feel you're being understood.

Four, you can reinforce your feeling of assertiveness by remembering to reach out and shake hands firmly when meeting people.

Five, you can increase your assertiveness in conversation by being sure not to use questions to replace statements. Consider, for example, the remarks below.

Arthur to Diane: "Would you like to cover your kitchen floor with purple linoleum?"

Susan to Everett: "Is it too cold for you?"

Both are passive, nonassertive comments. The following statements express what is really meant.

Arthur to Diane: "I'd love to see your kitchen floor covered with purple linoleum."

Susan to Everett: "I'm freezing!"

DAY THIRTEEN CHECKLIST

1. To become more assertive:
   - Use such phrases as "I think," "I believe" more frequently.
   - Use short, simple sentences.
   - Look the person you're talking to in the eyes.
   - Reach out to shake hands.
   - Don't substitute questions for statements.
2. To improve in expressing emotions:
   - Practice with a friend.
   - Adopt a better-late-than-never principle.

DAY FOURTEEN

Goals

We talked before about the sense of mastery that comes with stopping smoking for many men and women, and how the skills learned in the process can be used in other life experiences. Working toward goals is another benefit that can result and that, similarly, will stand you in good stead in many areas of your life from now on.

The steps that you've been taking to achieve your goal of becoming free from tobacco (making a decision, identifying obstacles and planning strategies ahead of time, rehearsing, reflecting and so forth) can work to propel you forward to the attainment of other goals as well. Today we'd like to give you some more principles for successfully working toward goals. As you read these guidelines, consider first how they apply to your recent success in becoming a non-smoker. Then you may want to consider other goals you'd like to pursue and decide which will be the next goal you'll work toward. Once you've decided on it, you can think about the suggestions below as they pertain to this next high-priority goal.

One, base your goals on your values. Your decision to stop smoking, for instance, may have been based on valuing life, or health or being in control. Or perhaps smoking seemed to you a "dirty, ugly habit" that offended your aesthetic values.

Two, have a vision of yourself as having already succeeded at your goal. You might, for example, have a vision of yourself as a relaxed non-smoker of many years. Someone who can create a strong image of eventual success from the time he or she starts working toward a new goal is far more likely to succeed in actuality. The vision should be as vivid as possible: try to truly picture yourself in living color going about your daily life, happily and peacefully, as a successful non-smoker.

Three, use long-range goals to enable you to attain short-term ones. For instance, your toughing it out through the early days of abstinence from tobacco was no doubt made possible by the long-range goal you had in mind. Cramming for exams is endurable to many students only because they have a clear image of what success and graduation will mean to them. Tackling a truly grimy room may similarly require the inspiration of a sparkling vision of the room spanking clean.

Four, define the kind and amount of work that is required to attain your goal and compare that to previous efforts. People can fail to achieve their goals because they don't have a realistic expectation of what is required to succeed.

Five, take yourself seriously and communicate that

seriousness to other people. The more you convince others that you believe in your goal, the more likely they are to take you seriously and give you constructive support. "I quit smoking *again!*", for example, is a remark that would be unlikely to win you much positive reinforcement.

Today makes two weeks since you stopped smoking. Have you made sure that everybody knows about it? If you chose to keep those first few days to yourself, maybe it's time you let the word out now. You deserve all the compliments you can recruit, so grab a megaphone and announce your achievement to the world!

DAY FOURTEEN CHECKLIST

1. Base your goals on your values.
2. Have a strong vision of yourself as having already succeeded at your goal.
3. Use long-range goals to enable you to attain short-term ones.
4. Define realistically what needs to be done to succeed.
5. Communicate to others that you are serious about your goal.

DAY FIFTEEN

Long-Term Benefits

In the last couple of days we've been talking about some of the important fringe benefits of becoming a non-smoker. You're starting your third week off cigarettes now and it's time to begin not so much turning your attention *away* from cigarettes as directing your attention *toward* other, positive issues like mastering situations, becoming more assertive and planning ahead to pursue other goals. Today, though, we want to come back to the extraordinary physical reality of what you are achieving in stopping smoking. We want to review the long-term health benefits to yourself, your loved ones and your community.

We could have started this *FreshStart* book with a look at the enormous health risks of smoking and the improvements you will gain by stopping. We knew, though, that most smokers had already heard at least part of this information, and that these facts were probably what led you to decide to kick the tobacco dependency. Let's face it: regardless of what was in the forefront of your mind as an incentive to quit smoking, not many of you would even have considered stopping if cigarettes were not hazardous to your health.

We've already considered a few of the quick rewards of stopping smoking; let's look now at some of the many, many long-term gains.

Cigarette smoking is the leading cause of chronic obstructive lung disease, which includes chronic bronchitis and emphysema. The progressive loss of lung function that characterizes this disease causes shortness of breath, which in turn reduces the level of physical activity. In fact, the degree of reduced activity is greater in chronic obstructive lung disease than in any other major disease. Beginning after a few years of smoking, some smokers develop abnormal lung function, and their lung function continues to decline as long as they go on smoking. But when the smoker quits, as *you* have, the rate of functional decline slows significantly. *No matter how long they've smoked and even if they already have emphysema, disability and discomfort are reduced and longevity is increased when they stop*. For smokers who do not yet have emphysema but who do have chronic bronchitis, it is likely that the condition will disappear completely when their smoking ends.

Cigarette smoking is responsible for 83 percent of all lung cancer cases. And for *all kinds of cancer*, the death rate for male smokers is twice that for male non-smokers; the rate is 67 percent higher for female smokers than for female non-smokers. Overall, smoking accounts for almost one-third of all cancer deaths. Cigarettes have been specifically implicated in cancers of the bladder, esophagus, larynx, lung, mouth, pancreas and pharynx, and data are accumulating on the relationship of tobacco to still other kinds of cancer.

Sex differences in lung cancer mortality have narrowed as a result of increased smoking among women born between 1920 and 1940. In 1985, lung cancer rates for the first time surpassed breast cancer rates as the leading cause of cancer deaths among women. Lung cancer mortality for women will continue to climb for at least the next two decades unless there are extraordinary increases in the percentage of women who stop smoking.

Your risk for lung cancer decreases gradually over time once you've given up smoking. *With every year that you are a non-smoker your risk for lung cancer goes down significantly*, until, after an average of thirteen years, your risk for lung cancer approaches that of someone who has never smoked.

The association between cardiovascular disease and smoking is also proven. Cigarette smoking is the leading risk factor for death from cardiovascular disease. *The single most important thing that a person who has suffered a heart attack can do to prevent another, possibly fatal, attack is to stop smoking*. Similarly, stopping smoking is a sure way to help *prevent* the onset of cardiovascular disease. And as we've said before, the reduction in risk for heart disease begins at once with the last puff of a cigarette.

Putting together the risks for all of these major diseases (which together constitute only the tip of the iceberg in terms of the *number* of diseases linked to cigarette smoking), it turns out that, for example, a non-smoker can expect to live over seven years longer than a thirty-year-old male smoker: a difference in longevity that no one could call trivial.

Moreover, when you stop smoking, you make a remarkable contribution to the health of others as well. It is well known that children raised in a home with one or more smokers have significantly greater incidences of allergic and respiratory problems. Not only that, but recent data suggest that non-smoking women whose husbands smoke are at greater risk of dying from heart disease than wives of non-smokers. Equally disturbing are recent data indicating that if you live with a smoker, you can double your odds of developing lung cancer.

People who have preexisting heart or lung diseases are particularly vulnerable to "passive" or "involuntary" smoking—the exposure of non-smokers to tobacco combustion from other people's cigarettes. But even healthy adults are at increased risk for heart and lung diseases after chronic exposure to other people's smoking. Moreover, the great majority of non-smokers as well as a good number of smokers find that being in a room, car or other space contaminated by tobacco smoke is unpleasant and irritating.

In summary, your personal achievement in quitting constitutes a major contribution to yourself, your family and friends and the community in which you live— to the comfort, quality of life and longevity of all of the people you spend time with.

DAY FIFTEEN CHECKLIST

1. Your long-term benefits of stopping smoking include, among many others:
   - Increased longevity
   - Reduced disability and discomfort from chronic obstructive lung disease
   - Reduced risk of lung cancer
   - Reduced risk of cardiovascular disease
   - Reduced risk of a second heart attack
   - Reduced risk of a fatal heart attack
2. Involuntary smoking has been shown to:
   - Increase respiratory and allergic conditions among children of smokers
   - Increase death from heart disease among non-smoking wives of smokers
   - Double the lung cancer rates among non-smoking persons who live with smokers
   - Irritate and annoy both non-smokers and smokers

DAY SIXTEEN

Psychosocial Dependency— The Final Hook

We spent a lot of time in the earlier part of this *FreshStart* program describing and suggesting strategies for dealing with tobacco withdrawal. This early emphasis on the chemical addiction hook of smoking was made not because it's the most difficult to break (for the majority of smokers, it's not), but because it's the first hook that needs to be dealt with. If withdrawal symptoms are going to occur, they will appear immediately, in the first few days off cigarettes. There *are* individuals for whom chemical addiction is the most difficult factor: these are generally people who have a terrible time making it through even twenty-four hours without a cigarette, and are often very heavy smokers. The great news for this group of men and women, though, is that they are quite likely to stay off cigarettes once they've made it through withdrawal. The battle for them is fought in the first few days, and when it's won, their smoking problem is often over and done with. Friends of these particularly addicted, heavy-smoking individuals are often amazed to see how quickly they became smoke-free!

Most smokers, though, do *not* have a terrible withdrawal period. And as we've said, the habit components of smoking is for almost all smokers the easiest hook to break. Why, then, do so many men and women return to cigarettes after stopping? The answer is the third and final hook of tobacco: psychosocial dependency.

After years of smoking, cigarettes come to take on a variety of personal and social meanings. We've discussed some of these already, for example that cigarettes may come to be experienced as a way of dealing with anger. Some of the meanings that cigarettes take on for smokers are highly individualized: others come from the environment and especially from social myths perpetuated by tobacco advertising. For instance, many smokers use cigarettes to relax or take a break or make transitions from one activity to another. These practices are to a significant degree reinforced by illusions created by cigarette advertising and promotion.

Some of the principles we've already discussed, like increasing assertiveness and developing and enjoying a sense of mastery, address a variety of situations of psychosocial dependency. Today we are going to describe some additional psychosocial factors that hook people to their cigarettes.

Loneliness

Cigarettes become "friends" for some men and women. Smoking is a source of comfort in that it represents the familiar, something that is always there and can always be counted on. Experiencing cigarettes in this way is not at all unusual. Some new non-smokers find it helpful, in fact, to consciously allow themselves to go through a mourning period for their cigarettes, to permit themselves to grieve just as they would for a friend who had died. Other non-smokers focus instead on reminding themselves that cigarettes are like a friend who has betrayed them and therefore are their friends no longer. This, too, may require a period of grieving. In either case, the idea is that it is all right to feel sad for a while about saying goodbye to cigarettes. However, the most constructive steps that you can take, if you do miss cigarettes as friends, are those that directly address the experience of loneliness. Strategies that some other non-smokers have found to help them make the transition from smoking to non-smoking without falling victim to loneliness include: writing a letter to an old friend, reading a book, going for frequent walks in different neighborhoods and, perhaps most important, reaching out to make new friends.

Fear of Failure

Fear of failing to stay off cigarettes is a reason that some people do fail at it. Fear of failure is an obstacle for a number of reasons, but one of the most common is a perceived loss of esteem. You may have been receiving loads of congratulations and compliments on stopping smoking, with the result that the fear of disappointing other people and risking loss of their respect drives you back to smoking. A related reason is that you may want so badly to stay off cigarettes forever that you cannot tolerate the possibility that you might never do so. The reasoning here goes like this: if you were to apply full effort to staying off cigarettes and then fail, it would be a devastating admission to yourself that you might never be able to stop. But if you do not commit yourself fully now, the possibility remains that you can stop successfully at some point in the future. More simply put, the thought is that it's better not to try too hard, because then you might discover you can't kick tobacco after all.

The reassuring response to this thought is that there is no such thing as never being able to stop smoking. If you do fail, that failure does not reflect on your overall ability; rather, it suggests that you were not yet prepared to counter the many environmental and social factors that can make stopping difficult, which is certainly understandable. Just continue to prepare to overcome these difficulties as you encounter them in the next two to three months. You'll probably also find that your sense of self-esteem is less easily threatened, and even enhanced, when you're applying full effort in working toward the goal of remaining a non-smoker.

Loss of Sense of Identity

Some men and women feel that they're giving up part of their identity when they stop smoking. Joy, a secretary in Detroit, remembers that she felt that she wasn't herself without "my red pack of *Winstons* in one hand and my lighted cigarette in the other. . . . That's who people knew me as, a *Winston* smoker." Dave, a computer salesperson, tells how he initially "felt funny when I'd go into a meeting [with a client]—It used to be I'd open my briefcase and the first thing you'd see was a full carton of *Marlboros;* I'd always have a brand new carton in there. Then, after I'd quit, I'd sit down, open up my briefcase and there wouldn't be anything in there except what we were working on! I felt . . . empty-handed."

The identity loss that Joy and Dave felt disappeared on its own within two or three months; this is what generally happens. Sometimes, though, the person, not realizing that this feeling of identity loss is a temporary experience, succumbs to it and returns to smoking. If you experience your stopping smoking as taking away part of your identity, you can speed up the time it takes to shake this feeling by concentrating on other aspects of your identity. Here's an exercise you might enjoy.

Try listing some of the following in the margins of this book: your favorite movies, foods, animals, vacation places, colors and songs; your hobbies as a child and your hobbies now; the names of your closest friends; your occupation; where you were born; the names of your children; the names of your pets; how you spent your last two weekends, and so forth. Add some ideas of your own.

Now write down some of the following, in short phrases: what personality qualities you like most about yourself; what personality qualities you think other people appreciate most about you; how you would like your life to be more enjoyable five years from now (this may require several short phrases).

Finally, if you're in a philosophical mood, try using short phrases to describe your most important values.

Now go back, read what you've written in the margins, and reflect and elaborate on your sense of your own identity. After doing this for a while, we're sure you'll find that *there's so much there* that you don't really need the unnecessary clutter of cigarettes.

DAY SIXTEEN CHECKLIST

1. If cigarettes were your "friends," bury them, mourn them briefly, and then make new friends.
2. If you fear failure at staying off cigarettes, apply full effort to succeeding. Remember that failure this time means only that you were not fully prepared for this difficult task.
3. Focus on various aspects of your sense of identity, both deeper and closer to the surface.

DAY SEVENTEEN

Your New Identity as a Non-Smoker

You may have noticed that sometimes we refer to you as a non-smoker and sometimes as an ex-smoker. You are, of course, both. Since smoking will not be an issue of any kind in your life much longer, it doesn't, for the most part, matter which term you apply to yourself. Your smoking status will not be on your mind as frequently in the future as it may be now. There is some symbolic significance to the choice of terms, however, and we'd like to call this to your attention. As you'll see, either non-smoker or ex-smoker is a fine term, depending on how you mean it.

Some people believe that no matter how long they go without smoking, cigarettes will always be a part of their lives in some way; some people even feel that in some fundamental way they will always be smokers, even though they don't smoke. This is a false and dangerous way of thinking. The danger is that these

139

thoughts can easily become self-fulfilling prophecies. The world is filled with images of smoking, not to mention quite a few smokers. If you believe that you are still part of this smoking world, then it's only natural to respond to all this environmental stimulation by starting to smoke again. Individuals who feel this way often refer to themselves as *ex*-smokers; this term seems more connected to smoking than does *non*-smoker. It's as though the "ex" is shorthand for "not smoking at the moment, but don't hold your breath."

Other men and women no longer identify themselves as smokers, but they feel they don't deserve to call themselves *non*-smokers because this implies that they have never smoked. It's as though they feel they should punish themselves for their past mistake by continuing to call attention to it. But we would like to stress here, for those of you to whom this issue applies, that starting smoking was not *your* mistake. If you're like most smokers, you were not even an adult when you became addicted to, habituated to and psychosocially dependent on tobacco. You took your cues from the world around you and they told you that smoking was a harmless, enjoyable, relaxing social habit engaged in by pleasure-loving social beings like yourself. You are, of course, an adult now, and we're sure you're aware of how false those early images of smoking were. However, from now on if you don't stay off cigarettes, *that* may be a mistake for which you are responsible.

You are a *non*-smoker, regardless of how long you've been off cigarettes. We're stating this so strongly that you may wonder why we say it can also be fine to use the term *ex*-smoker. Here, then, is another symbolic meaning of that term. Some people love saying "I'm an *ex*-smoker!" because every time they say it, they feel again a sense of pride in having conquered to-bacco. They may be men and women who feel totally confident that they will never smoke again, and they take great pleasure in letting people know about their enormous achievement. So, as you can see, non-smoker and ex-smoker are both terrific terms for you to use. Both terms are accurate, and either one should be music to the ears of anyone who has conquered cigarettes.

There is one more, related "identity" topic that we'd like to discuss with you. A few smokers subscribe to the myth that the longing for cigarettes will never go away. These people have usually heard of someone who quit smoking twenty years ago and claims still to desire cigarettes every single day. There are such individuals, but they are few and far between, and their problem has nothing to do with the power of cigarettes. Of the many problems linked to smoking, virtually all are the fault of the cigarettes and not the smokers; this is the one exception. The person who clings to the memory of cigarettes is like someone who still yearns for a lost lover of twenty years ago; their problem is one of living in the past. People who quit smoking do *not* always long for cigarettes. For you, as for them, smoking will soon be past history in every way.

DAY SEVENTEEN CHECKLIST

1. Think of why you feel good about being able to refer to yourself as an *ex*-smoker.
2. Think of why you feel good about being able to refer to yourself as a *non*-smoker.
3. Remind yourself that smoking will soon be past history for you.

DAY EIGHTEEN

Reinforcement

You've done it! You've really stopped smoking. We suggest you spend some time today reinforcing your success. Here are some ways to do that.

First, starting with Day One, Quit Day, use the checklist at the end of each chapter to review everything you've done so far. Any time you don't recall the details of a point that the checklist refers to, go back to the text of the chapter and review it. As you go over each day's chapter, remind yourself of how many strategies you've employed, how many issues you've reflected on and how many obstacles you've countered to get where you are today. This review of your recent efforts will reinforce your achievement.

Second, when you get to Day Ten, allow a moment to consider your current weight status. If you've gained no weight since stopping smoking, terrific; move on to the next chapter for review. If you have gained a pound or two, however, please go back and go over that chapter in detail. Allow yourself time to really consider the different possible reasons for gaining weight after stopping smoking and the kinds of strategies that can be effective in countering that weight gain. Think of how you've been spending the last two and a half weeks. Have you been physically active? If you have gained any weight and can't figure out why, even after reviewing the chapter for Day Ten, do two things: One, add twenty minutes a day of moderate exercise to the exercise you're currently getting. Two, eat 350 fewer calories a day.

As additional fuel to reinforce your effort at losing this weight right away, we've provided a quick calorie counter. This brief list includes both nutritious foods and some not-so-nutritious ones. This quick calorie counter is not a recommended eating list but rather a sampling of some of the foods that an average American might eat at, or between, meals. Remember, we're not suggesting you count the calories of everything you eat (unless you want to); just find a way to eliminate 350 calories a day.

QUICK CALORIE COUNTER

FOOD ITEM	CALORIES
American processed cheese (1 oz.)	105
Angel food cake (1 slice)	135
Apple (1 medium)	80
Apple juice (½ cup)	60
Asparagus (4 spears)	15
Avocado (1 medium)	370
Bacon (2 slices)	85
Bagel (1 medium)	165
Bean sprouts (½ cup)	16

Beef burrito (1 serving)	466
Beef, ground, broiled (3 oz.)	235
Beer (12 oz.)	150
Beer, light (12 oz.)	105
Blackeyed peas (½ cup)	95
Bran muffin (1 medium)	110
Brussels sprouts (½ cup)	28
Butter (1 pat)	35
Buttermilk (1 cup)	100
Catsup (1 tb.)	15
Cheddar cheese (1 oz.)	115
Chef's salad (2½ cups)	546
Chicken, broiled (3.5 oz.)	130
Chicken, fried (3 oz.)	208
Chocolate cake with icing (3″ square)	365
Chocolate pudding (½ cup)	160
Chow mein and noodles (1¼ cup)	310
Clams or oysters, raw (3 oz.)	65
Coffee or tea, plain (1 cup)	2
Corn (1 ear, 5″)	70
Corn or bran flakes (1 cup)	95
Cream (1 tb.)	20
Cream cheese (2 tb.)	100
Cucumber (7 slices)	5
Danish pastry (4″ piece)	275
Diet soda (12 oz.)	1
Doughnut, cake-type (1 medium)	164
Egg, fried or scrambled (1)	85
Egg, hard-boiled (1)	80
Fish stick (1 medium)	50
Gin, 80 proof (1½ oz.)	95
Graham crackers (2)	55
Grapefruit juice (½ cup)	48

DAY EIGHTEEN

Gravy (¼ cup)	164
Green beans (½ cup)	15
Grits (½ cup)	63
Honey (1 tb.)	65
Ice cream (½ cup)	135
Jell-O (½ cup)	70
Lamb chop, broiled (3 oz.)	360
Lettuce (½ cup)	5
Lima beans (½ cup)	130
Manicotti with meat sauce (1 serving)	560
Margarine (1 pat)	35
Mayonnaise (1 tb.)	100
Milkshake (1 cup)	244
Milk, skimmed (1 cup)	85
Milk, whole (1 cup)	150
Oatmeal (½ cup)	65
Onion rings, fried (8)	300
Pancakes with syrup (3)	355
Peaches, canned, in syrup (½ cup)	100
Peanut butter (1 tb.)	95
Peanuts (¼ cup)	210
Peas (½ cup)	75
Pecan pie (1 slice)	495
Pizza, cheese (1 slice of 12″ pie)	145
Pizza, pepperoni (1 slice of 12″ pie)	315
Popcorn (1 cup)	40
Pork sausage (1 link—½ oz.)	60
Potato, baked (1 medium)	145
Potato chips (10)	115
Rice (½ cup)	113
Rye bread (1 slice)	60
Saltine crackers (2)	25

Sandwiches

Cheeseburger	459
Club	591
Egg salad	400
Hamburger	354
Hot roast beef with gravy	509
Hot turkey with gravy	486
Peanut butter and jelly	385
Pork barbecue	270
Submarine or hoagie (11″ long)	907
Tuna salad	315

Soups (1 cup):

Bean and pork	170
Beef broth	30
Chicken noodle	55
Lentil	125
Split pea	145
Tomato	90
Sour cream (1 tb.)	25
Spinach (½ cup)	23
Steak, broiled (6 oz.)	345
Strawberries, fresh (½ cup)	28
Sugar (1 tsp.)	15
Sugar-coated corn flakes (1 cup)	155
Sweet potato, baked (1 medium)	160
Taco (1)	186
Tofu (1 cake, 2½″ × 2¾″ × 1″)	86
Tomato, fresh (½)	13
Vegetable oil (1 tb.)	120
Waffle with syrup (1)	292
Wheat germ (1 tb.)	25
White bread (1 slice)	70

| Whole wheat bread (1 slice) | 65 |
| Wine (3½ oz.) | 85 |

Calorie table developed by Betsy Haughton, Ed.D., R.D., Consultant on Nutrition to the American Cancer Society.

A third way to reinforce your non-smoking is by even more sharing with friends. Occasionally, new ex-smokers mention that they don't feel they've gotten enough praise. Often all the compliments come in the first week, and then friends seem to forget about your achievement. We suggest you not wait for compliments; instead, initiate them yourself. This is the time to be talking about what you've accomplished for yourself and others by stopping smoking. It's important that you talk about it as much as you can for a month or so, because a time will come when it may be best to quit talking about it, at least on a regular basis: part of being smoke-free forever is to pretty much forget about smoking. You won't need to deliberately try to suppress thoughts about cigarettes; in fact, that would be counter-productive. Rather, the thoughts will vanish on their own except for occasional fleeting, harmless thoughts. But in the meantime your new non-smoking status still needs attention to reinforce it, and your tremendous achievement still deserves recognition. So why not just say to your neighbor or someone at your office: "Do you realize this is my eighteenth smoke-free day?" Or sit down with your partner and say, "I really want to tell you again what stopping smoking means to me. I'm so proud of it, I can't get it out of my mind."

Fourth, you might want to consider wearing a pin,

T-shirt or button to announce your new success to everyone who sees you. Or perhaps place a polite "Thank You for Not Smoking" placard on your desk or table or kitchen counter. The pins and T-shirts can be fun and the placard helpful both for you and the people reading it.

Fifth and finally, review the benefits of stopping smoking that have rippled into other areas of your life. Has your tennis game improved because of the extra practice you've been putting in? Has your self-confidence been shining? One woman, for example, credits stopping smoking with winning her a big promotion in the museum where she works. Jackie explains: "I was just so confident about everything—how could they turn me down?" Did all the water you've been drinking lead to fresher-looking skin? Do you wake up feeling healthier and thus get a more energetic start on your day?

DAY EIGHTEEN CHECKLIST

1. Review Days One through Seventeen.
2. Begin to correct any weight gain this week.
3. Initiate sharing with friends.
4. Try buttons, T-shirts and placards.
5. Review ripple benefits of not-smoking.

DAY NINETEEN

Planning for a Crisis

Let us be clear from the start that when we say "crisis" we mean the death of a loved one, a major flood in your home, a highway accident or comparable life event. We are not talking about daily stresses like being stuck in rush-hour traffic, having a bad day at the office or having a quarrel with your lover. These daily stresses *are* more likely to lead you back to smoking than are crises. This is largely a matter of timing, in that a real crisis is not likely to occur during your first three weeks of not smoking, when you are most vulnerable, whereas minor irritations and stresses occur to most of us frequently, if not every day. Why then aren't we talking about the minor stresses rather than the major crises?

The truth is we *have* been talking about the minor stresses. Most of this *FreshStart* program has been about stress management, which is one of the keys to successfully stopping smoking and staying off cigarettes. Every one of the techniques in the program—

from deep breathing and the Floating Exercise to learning how to become more assertive as an alternative to suppressing anger and other emotions—is intended to help you manage daily stresses and frustrations as part of the process of becoming a non-smoker.

We turn today to a discussion of crises because of the unique role they can play in leading you to return to smoking, even when you've been successfully off cigarettes for some time.

It's unpleasant to think about tragedies and crises, and there's no need to dwell upon possible future events of this kind. It's important, though, to acknowledge that you will in the future experience a crisis of some kind. Someone you care about will become seriously ill or die, for example. And it's important *now*, not then, to consider what will prevent you from returning to smoking when a crisis occurs. What sometimes happens is that in a crisis you are hit suddenly with a wish for a cigarette, even though you may not have smoked or thought of cigarettes for some time. Equally often, however, another person involved in the crisis offers you a cigarette because he or she feels so powerless to help you and doesn't know what else to do. And you may take it, not because you want it but because you are in a passive or automatic state.

In the midst of a crisis, the issue of whether you smoke or not will likely seem trivial. Your attitude might even be fatalistic: "It doesn't matter what happens to me now." This, then, is your final task of *planning ahead* to stay off cigarettes: there are two things you can do *today* to prepare yourself not to smoke when you experience a crisis in the future.

The first is to continue to ritualize your personal statement of commitment. Do you look at your card with the single sentence on it daily? Do you repeat the statement to yourself several times each day? You needn't continue to do this forever—just for the remaining three days of your *FreshStart* program. By your twenty-first day of non-smoking, the statement of commitment should be a solid automatic response. In a crisis you may not be able even to try to remember why you didn't want to smoke; an automatic response, such as your personal statement of commitment, can spring into your mind spontaneously and effortlessly.

A second strategy to employ now that can help you in the distant future is to think of why you wouldn't want to smoke, no matter what crisis occurred. A thought that a lot of people find helpful is that "smoking can't make anything better, and it can make a lot of things worse." Another expression that some individuals have found helpful is "I'll make it through this crisis somehow; I don't want to come out of it as a smoker again." You may have other more personal thoughts that seem meaningful. The idea is to use the rational state you're in now to think through an issue that in a crisis you might have only an irrational response available for.

Do you have your "Planning Ahead" list handy? (See Day Nine.) We suggest you add "crisis" to the list of possible obstacles, and then enter your strategies for countering this obstacle.

DAY NINETEEN CHECKLIST

Plan ahead for a crisis in two ways:

1. Be sure you've turned your personal statement of commitment into an automatic response.
2. Consider now why you would not want to smoke even in the event of a crisis.

DAY TWENTY

Adding to Your Life

By stopping smoking you've added health and years to your life and no doubt to others' lives as well.

You've added taste and smell, and perhaps some new favorite herbs, foods, flowers and colognes in the process.

You've added energy and stamina; if you've been strictly adhering to this *FreshStart* program, you've added more brisk walking or time at your favorite sport.

You've added a lot of water to your life, at least temporarily.

The list of what you've added in these past nineteen days goes on and on. You may have set new goals and started working on them. You may have added a greater degree of assertiveness than you had previously experienced. You've added deep breathing, a relaxation exercise and maybe a lot of fresh raw vegetables (please stick with these vegetables, and fruit, too!). You've added so much to your life that you must be on a roll. This being the case, we'd like to ask you now to think of additional ways to enhance your enjoyment of life.

We'd like you to consider ways that you can add to your life in each of three categories. We suggest you approach this rewarding task by sharing your thoughts and feelings on each of these topics with someone you care about or by writing them down. This is a happy assignment, and one which you can approach in an expansive mood.

Here are the three categories.

Your family and friends. With the concept of "adding to" in mind, consider your family and friends. You can think of this concept both in terms of giving to individual friends and family members and of adding new friends and even family members!

Your hobbies and avocations. The concept of hobbies is frequently trivialized. But in fact people's hobbies often reflect their strongest interests, and these activities may be among their most pleasurable times. From another perspective, today's hobby may turn out to be tomorrow's career. Consider how you can add to your enjoyment of your current hobbies and avocations, and what new hobbies you can add to your life.

Your inner world. Among the ways in which you can enrich your inner world are adding laughter (when you laugh, you're often in touch with your deepest self); spending more time reflecting on your life experiences; becoming more involved with philosophical or religious matters. Take your time with this category, and return to this task from time to time with more thoughts on how you can add to your inner world.

DAY TWENTY

You may need to exert some deliberate control in maintaining your non-smoking for a few more weeks. To a significant extent, though, it's time to be getting on with your life. Succeeding at non-smoking means letting go both of cigarettes and of thoughts about cigarettes. Focusing on the positive additions to your life—those you've already made and those you want to make in the future—can be a stimulating and pleasurable way to ease yourself away from cigarettes in every sense.

DAY TWENTY CHECKLIST

1. Review all that you've added to your life in these past twenty days.
2. Write down or discuss with a friend the additions you can make in these three categories:
   - Family and friends
   - Hobbies and avocations
   - Your inner world

DAY TWENTY-ONE

Celebration and Commitment

No more single-candle celebrations! You've succeeded in conquering tobacco and it's time for an all-out bash! Plan your celebration for tonight, now; alter your schedule or previous plans, if necessary. Have you ever thrown a party at the last minute? Tonight might be the time to do just that. On the other hand, for some people the grandest celebration in the world would be a free evening all to themselves, with no responsibilities to anyone. Can you arrange that? Perhaps your family can make that their celebration present to you.

You've made it to day twenty-one! Over two-thirds of all recidivism (returning to smoking) takes place before the third week of non-smoking, so you've already joined the majority of successful ex-smokers. And you have planned for the next couple of months with strategies for any obstacles you might encounter, though it's unlikely you'll have any major hurdles ahead of you. Keep your *FreshStart* book with you for at least another three weeks, so that you can refer to it in case of an emergency—an unexpected obstacle. And continue to practice the techniques to manage stress and to manage your weight for about the same period of time, or for as long as needed.

Some of you may still be struggling or may even have slipped and taken a cigarette recently. As we have said before, we urge you not to focus on these slips but rather to move forward with even greater determination. Allow yourself a little more time each day to review the parts of the *FreshStart* program that you think might be most helpful to you and to do the tasks or exercises suggested. Especially create that vision of yourself tobacco-free: make it a vivid, compelling vision and keep it in front of you as much of the time as you can.

There is a still worse possibility: maybe you've been smoking quite a bit in these first three weeks. In that case, our suggestion is a different one; if you've had more than two or three cigarettes, then we'd like you to focus very much on your smoking. Your return to smoking was a recent event, so try to recall as clearly as possible what the events were that led up to your smoking, and especially what you were feeling and thinking when you reached for a cigarette. Then refer to the particular parts of the *FreshStart* program that address these obstacles. If, in fact, you've barely quit smoking at all, we suggest you do go back to the Introduction and begin the program again. However, since you're already familiar with the strategies, do two days at a time. Most of all remember that you've got lots of company. Most longtime non-smokers tried without success before reaching their goal eventually.

Most of the benefits of your success in stopping smoking are yet to come, although we've described many of them to you. One benefit that you can already experience, though you may appreciate it more fully in the future, is that of your newfound freedom. You've not only attained freedom from the damaging effects of tobacco, you've achieved freedom from addiction, habit and psychosocial dependency. At the time of this writing, the tobacco industry in the United States spends over *three billion dollars a year* advertising and promoting these three hooks of smoking. Along with your great personal victory, you've also scored a point on behalf of other aspiring non-smokers by demonstrating that one more person has said "no" to tobacco, and that they can do the same.

DAY TWENTY-ONE CHECKLIST

Congratulations! You've just achieved a major victory—you've finished this program successfully and started a healthy, smoke-free life.
